Steve Dobson

UNUSUAL HOTELS
OF THE WORLD

JONGLEZ

Far from seeking out luxury or charming hotels that are often inaccessible to ordinary mortals because they are prohibitively expensive and then turn out to be soulless, unwelcoming places, the "Unusual Hotels of the World" guide lists 50 hotels around the world with exceptional features, astonishingly original and out of the ordinary. We've taken great pleasure in carefully choosing hotels with extremely high standards that know how to surprise you with their utter uniqueness. Catering for all budgets (from 20 euros to over 1,000 euros per night), the places alone are very often worth the trip and will certainly make your stay unforgettable.

We sincerely hope that you'll enjoy visiting them as much as we did! Bon voyage!

Americas

Europe

Asia, Oceania, Africa

Ice Hotel Quebec

North America joins the Ice Hotel family

Sister of the original Icehotel in Jukkasjärvi (Sweden), Ice Hotel Quebec-Canada offers probably the easiest access to ice room accommodation of any snow or ice property today. Situated just outside Quebec City, with easy road and public transport connections, this 2,800 m² (30,000 sq. ft) resort is built next to Station Duchesnay, an existing tourist centre. Taking around five weeks to build using 15,000 tons of snow and 500 tons of ice, it is open from early January to early April – a little over three months. Architecturally it is stunning, with vaulted ceilings over 5 m (18 ft) high held up by columns of ice, ice carvings and snow sculptures in the different rooms, bar and chapel.

Ice rooms are simply decorated and, if your budget allows, you should consider the theme suites, especially one of the two with its own fireplace. These suites have ice sculptures and carvings inside and are lit by candle-light. A couple of the suites have access to the jacuzzi spa and sauna outside for evening stargazing too.

Access to the room is provided from 9 pm to 8 am after the tourists have left, however you are provided with a warm luggage area within the Ice Hotel complex during the afternoon. Toilet and washing facilities are also provided in this area. All meals are served in the adjoining hotel, but the ice bar is open from early evening for an aperitif or nightcap.

To do

Next door to the Ice Hotel complex itself is Station Duchesnay with winter sports facilities including dog sledding and cross-country skiing. Quebec City, 40 minutes by car, has been designated a World Heritage site by UNESCO and is the only walled city in North America. It is filled with interesting shops and exhibitions – few more interesting than the Ursulines Museum, part of the original monastery located on Donnaconna Street (near St-Louis). The Ursuline order of nuns landed in Quebec in 1639 and founded the first girls' school in North America. The museum traces the history and showcases their art, embroidery, life and work.

Ice Hotel Quebec-Canada
143, route Duchesnay Pavillon Regie
Sainte-Catherine-de-la-Jacques-Cartier
QC, Canada G0A 3M0
+1 (0)418 875 4522
information@icehotel-canada.com
www.icehotel-canada.com
Thirty-six double rooms and suites

Rates and location From CAN$ 299 plus tax per person per night based on double occupancy. Specific theme rooms are extra. Reduced rates apply to children. Located on the site of the Station Touristique Duchesnay on the shores of Lake St Joseph, it is about 40 km (25 miles) north-west of the city centre. The complex has easy access by car, bus or taxi.

King Pacific Lodge

Floating luxury in Canadian wilderness

While floating hotels are not an original idea, often they are based around a rushed conversion of an existing barge or the liberty ships of the 1950s. Unwilling to squeeze guests into a refit of an existing vessel, King Pacific Lodge owner Jo Morita decided to build this property from scratch. It helps that he is the son of the co-founder of Sony and, from his previous involvement with the Telluride mountain resort, understands how to satisfy the most demanding guest requests. Even so, the creation of King Pacific Lodge is peculiar to this part of the world and the attention to detail impressive.

Reached by a 2¼ hour floatplane transfer from Vancouver door-to-door, including a plane switch, few resorts have made the wilderness more accessible – while at the same time recognizing the need for environmentally aware practices. Uniquely, all visitor travels are offset as part of the overall package pricing, including flights and transit from the visitor's home anywhere in the world.

Flights arrive twice a week providing three-, four- or seven-night combination packages.

The facilities are equally impressive. Seventeen rooms offer wilderness or waterside views, with one suite offering both by spanning the property. Ocean views are usually the first to book, as they have sunset views but also any noise from waterside activity. Wilderness views showcase the rainforest and are a haven of tranquility. Noise isn't an issue, as it's generally visitor generated and you're probably already out fly fishing, trekking or in a canoe somewhere during the day. There aren't any nightclubs or noisy neighbours!

King Pacific Lodge
Princess Royal Island
British Columbia
Canada
info@kingpacificlodge.com
www.kingpacificlodge.com
Seventeen rooms offering wilderness
or waterside views

Rates
Due to the requirement to fly guests direct
to the lodge, the minimum package is an all-inclusive
three-night stay from CAN$ 4,490 per person based
on double occupancy to family suites at CAN$ 11,390
per person. Some spa services, gratuities, taxes and
conservation charges are not included in these rates.

To do

Activities are seasonal like the food.
Summer months offer ocean fishing
for Chinook salmon, while in September
wildlife and fly fishing are at their
peak. All activities are included
apart from the specialized trips
and helicopter tours to see the rare
Ghost or Kermode bear. Helicopter trips
fly fishing are as spectacular as they
sound, and lessons are available.

Location
Arrive in Vancouver to pick up the chartered
floatplane for your $2\,1/4$ hour trip to the lodge.

Saugerties Lighthouse

See a slice of waterside history in this restored lighthouse

Lying off Hudson River, Saugerties Lighthouse offers a beautiful and unusual opportunity to step back to a less-rushed pace and more traditional way of life.

This 1869-built lighthouse fell into disuse in the 1950s and 60s as traffic reduced from the local port of Saugerties. With the automation of the light, the original building was neglected. A concerted campaign by the local villagers created a conservation trust, which was able to purchase the buildings and associated wetland reserve for a nominal $1 in return for their agreement to restore this landmark. In 1990, the light was restored and the doors opened to the public to share this slice of history.

Two second-floor rooms are provided for you to stay as a guest of the keeper, sharing bathroom and cooking facilities. Both offer views of the river and on sunny days, once the haze on the Hudson has lifted, you can see across to Albany and the distant Catskills mountain range. The only noise you'll hear is the comforting chugging of river traffic, or the distant ringing of the railroad bell as trains cross the Kingston/Rhinecliff bridge.

The lighthouse itself is constructed on an outlying spit of land, with a walk from where you leave your car. Breakfast is provided, and the current keeper Patrick is an excellent and friendly host and a keen cook. Ask for tips about his bread! Although you're welcome to use the cooking and barbeque facilities yourselves, most guests choose to eat in nearby Saugerties. There are good restaurants, many Zagat rated, and Patrick is helpful in recommending favourites.

There is no bar, so make sure you bring your own beer or wine. There are few things as annoying as watching a beautiful evening sky but forgetting to pack a chilled beer to enjoy as the sun sets.

Saugerties Lighthouse
168 Lighthouse Drive
Saugerties,
NY 12477 USA
+1 (0)845 247 0656
info@saugertieslighthouse.com
www.saugertieslighthouse.com
Two rooms in shared lodging with lighthouse keeper

Rates
Either of the two double rooms with breakfast costs from US$ 160 on weekdays, rising to US$ 175 at weekends. Additional guests are US$ 35. Supervised children and pets are welcome.

Location
Saugerties Lighthouse is a little over 40 miles from Albany NY by car. It can also be reached by Amtrak to nearby Rhinecliff or Hudson with a taxi ride to the lighthouse path. By boat – check with the keeper direct for details. It is worth travelling light, as you need to carry your belongings on foot along the gentle 1 km (1/2 mile) trail. A backpack is recommended.

To do

Wildlife is a central theme here,
with walks to the wetlands
for birdwatching and enjoying the fresh
air. Riverside activities include kayaking,
fishing and swimming in these calm
waters. You can once again find time
to think, however we recommend
you exercise your brain first before
venturing out onto the trails.

The wetlands are tidal, and some
of the outlying tracks can be underwater
for a few hours at extremes of high tide.
Check the tide tables provided before
you set out!

Jules' Undersea Lodge

Dive underwater to this two-roomed lodge

Jules' Undersea Lodge started out as the La Chalupa underwater research laboratory in the 1970s, and was one of the most advanced research habitats created. While special research projects are still undertaken, the running of the site now supports divers who wish to book either of two rooms for extended saturation stays underwater. The interior contains a central "moonpool" dive access and wet locker with hot showers. There is a shared kitchenette with fridge and microwave and a recreation area with books, music and videos. The rooms are 3 m (10 ft) long and 2 m (8 ft) in diameter, so adequate for a couple sleeping – as you're unlikely to bring too many heavy bags on the dive to your room.

The main feature of each room is the large, 106 cm (42 inch) round window that looks out into the sea. While you're looking out into the murky beyond, the fish are looking in at you. The mangrove lagoon in which Jules' is located is a natural nursery area for many reef fish. Tropical angelfish, parrotfish, barracuda and snappers peek in the windows of the habitat, while anemones, sponges, oysters and feather-duster worms seem to cover every inch of this underwater world. Guests explore their marine environment with scuba gear provided by the Lodge and are given an unlimited supply of tanks.

In order to comply with safety legislation, unqualified divers are required to take part in a 3 hour dive certification programme to ensure that they are aware of safety procedures underwater.

Jules' Undersea Lodge at Key Largo Undersea Park
51 Shoreland Drive
Key Largo, Florida 33037
USA
+1 (0)305 451 2353
info@jul.com
www.jul.com
Two underwater rooms for up to four guests in total

Rates
Overnight packages from US$ 345 to US$445 plus tax per person on a couple sharing basis.

To do

You can watch DVDs, videos and phone your friends, or even order a pizza or a wedding cake for underwater delivery. However, most guests are happy to look out into the lagoon and take in their undersea experience. A few favourite CDs are a nice addition to your diving kit.

Location
Jules' Undersea Lodge is located about 1½ hours'
drive from Miami International Airport at the bottom
of the Emerald Lagoon in Key Largo Undersea Park,
off Transylvania Avenue on the Overseas Highway
(mile marker 103.2). Note for visitors travelling by air,
a minimum 24 hours onshore is essential after your
stay underwater before flying.

Winvian

Sleep in a helicopter or in a tree

From when it was purchased in 1940, until it was transformed into an outlet for the artistic expression of fifteen professional architects, Winvian was the tranquil family farm of Winthrop and Vivian Smith. Over a weekend in 2001, the daughter and granddaughter team of Maggie and Heather Smith decided on a no-rules design competition to transform the property and eventually engaged the architects to build eighteen amazing cottages – each with a design history of its own.

From the bringing-outside-indoors approach of "Camping" to the rustic charm of "Woodlands", each cottage on the 46 hectare (113 acre) estate is completely unique, yet none more so than "Helicopter". Using a genuine US coastguard Sikorsky helicopter, rescued from Arizona, this cottage pays homage to the roots of Sikorsky in nearby Stratford. The helicopter dominates the room, with the cottage seemingly built around the outside. Even the rotor blades are embedded in the ceiling and walls. Inside the chopper is a bar and lounge area and, if the excitement of playing rescue eventually fades, a giant flatscreen TV to watch the latest action-movie releases on cable TV. Never was a mission more comfortable! Clamber into the flight deck, pull the control columns and flick the switches – scramble for rescue!

The bed is to the side of the room staring straight at the Sikorsky, showing a view that was once a welcome sight for those in distress. No worry of that here. The furnishings are of a high standard and, should you need help to regain your composure, a 5 minute walk to the spa will sooth any frayed nerves. Other cottages share equally impressive artistic credentials, although perhaps none with such technology on show. The double-deck treehouse, for example, oozes rustic charm, however as anyone building large structures in wood will attest – treehouses are models of engineering in their own right. Winvian underplays the amazing environment that it offers guests and the only regret is that they don't admit children under 18 to join in the fun.

Winvian
155 Alain White Road
Morris
Connecticut 06763
USA
Hsmith@winvian.com
www.winvian.com
Eighteen get-away cottages

Rates and location From US$ 1,450 to US$ 1,950 per cottage per night inclusive of all facilities, meals, soft drinks and some spirits and wine, with state sales taxes and service in addition. The helicopter cottage is middle-tier priced at US$ 1,700. Although Winvian is only a short distance off Route 63, it is tucked away down a couple of minor roads and you need to follow the directions or your satnav to find it.

To do

As if your luxury cottage wasn't
enough, the Winvian team provide
fly fishing and trekking gear, cross-
country skis and exercise equipment
should you be so inclined. While you
can't fly the helicopter in your
cottage, if you wanted lessons
they could surely be arranged.

Quinta Real Zacatecas

Bullring converted to luxury hotel

Beef is back on the menu at the Plaza de Toros San Pedro. While it no longer showcases the matador's skills, this bullring, built in 1866, faced demolition when it closed in 1975. Thankfully state laws recognized it as a historic monument, but it remained idle in a state of decay until Quinta Real started a two-year reconstruction, finally opening the hotel to guests in 1989. Accolades and plaudits from architects, travellers and those seeking an extraordinary venue, have followed the sympathetic reconstruction.

The city itself is a colonial attraction, with many historic and cultural sights, however, it is the bullring that dominates downtown.

Quinta Real Zacatecas is both a top-class hotel and historic monument in one. The rooms look inwards to the plaza and, although luxurious, are conservatively but comfortably furnished and cannot be considered unusual. The bar however starts to highlight the building's heritage, as it is located in the original bull pens. The tiered restaurant – a nightmare for waiters having to weave in and out of secluded alcove tables and up and down many staircases, is built into the original walls, where once crowds used to watch the spectacle. Now guests are more likely to preside over weddings and cultural events, using the bullring itself for dinners and gala spectacles.

To do

While the many cobbled streets of Zacatecas and historic buildings are the main draw to this UNESCO World Heritage site, take a ride on the cable car. It takes passengers over the town, from one of the old mines to the top of Cerro de la Bufa (2,666 m / 8,746 ft) high. The views of beautifully preserved pink stone buildings and the labyrinth of spotless narrow streets that twist and turn through the city are stunning, but not for those afraid of heights. Also check out the Gonzalez Ortega market for traditional leather and silverware gifts or jewellery.

Quinta Real Zacatecas
Av. Ignacio Rayón 434
Col. Centro, Zacatecas
Zac. 98000 Mexico
+492 (0)922 9104
www.quintareal.com
Forty-seven suites

Rates and location Offering forty-seven suites including an immense Presidential Suite – room prices vary with size and season, with junior doubles available from around US$ 180 per room per night inclusive of taxes, breakfast and service. Quinta Real Zacatecas is located 5 minutes from downtown, and a 20 minute ride from Zacatecas International Airport.

Canopy Tower Ecolodge and Nature Observatory

Radar tower hotel provides view of rainforest birds in tree canopy

Built in 1965 by the United States Air Force to house radar used in the defence of the Panama Canal, the tower was demilitarized and transferred to Panama in 1996. Located on top of Semaphore Hill, in the heart of the semi-deciduous Soberanía National Park, it rises above the tree canopy. Dominating the roof is the 9 m (30 ft) high geotangent dome with an observation deck surrounding it, from which you can see the Pacific entrance to the Panama Canal and the skyline of Panama City. The top floor is used as the main dining area, and is completely surrounded by panoramic windows. The second and first floors provide the living space, with en suite bathrooms and large windows to observe lower levels of the forest canopy.

You are never more than a short distance from the birds and should pack earplugs if you're a light sleeper and don't want to be woken at first light. They wake at dawn on this migratory route and you'll have ample opportunity to see those normally only glimpsed high in the tops of trees, right outside your Canopy Tower room.

Your host is the friendly Raúl Arias de Para, who not only is knowledgeable about the birds and wildlife but tells some great lighthearted stories over evening drinks.

Canopy Tower Ecolodge and Nature Observatory
Semaphore Hill - Semaphore Hill Road Soberanía
National Park - Panama
+1 (0)507 264 5720
birding@canopytower.com
www.canopytower.com
Twelve rooms in the tower.

Rates and location
From $US 125 per person per night on a couple sharing basis to $ 200 per person per night plus taxes, transportation and tips. Canopy Tower does not accommodate children younger than 13 years of age.

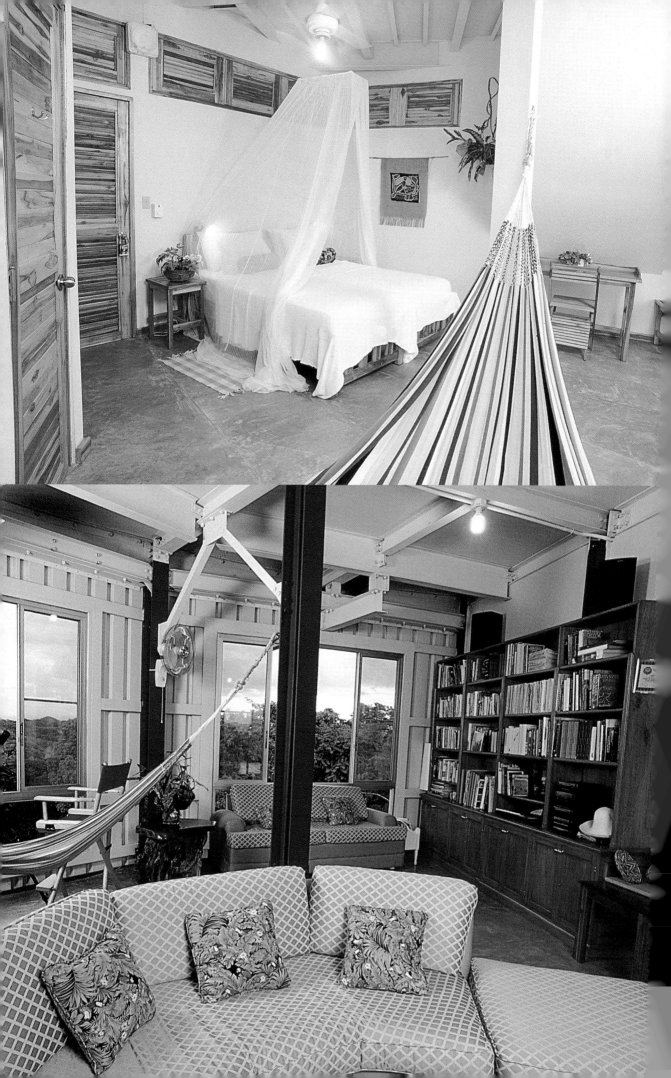

To do

If you're not a birdwatcher yourself,
then the activities of the Panama Canal
are likely to be the main attraction of
the area. There are two sets of locks on
the Pacific side of the canal, Miraflores
and Pedro Miguel, a short drive from
the Tower, as well as the Panama
Canal Visitor Centre. Panama City
itself is interesting and the Bridge
of Life building at the Museum
of Biodiversity, designed by Frank O.
Gehry, is scheduled to open in late 2007.
It promises to be another stunning
Gehry design and looks worth a visit

Exploranter

Hotel that moves around Latin America

A combination of coach and twenty-seven bedroom trailer, the Exploranter travelling hotel has completed more than 100 trips since 2001. The longest trip, covering 80,000 km took nearly a year and visited as far as Alaska. More often, the trips are based closer to their headquarters in São Paulo, visiting unexpected areas of Brazil as well as the spectacular regions of Patagonia and Atacama, in Argentina and Chile.

There are two parts to Exploranter; a day-coach and sleeping trailer. The day-coach seats thirty in facing sets of eight, so that while on the road these become small social areas. The coach is also equipped with professional catering facilities for up to 200. The attached trailer provides three shower-equipped bathrooms and twenty-seven sleeping compartments, each around 2 m long with comfortable semi-orthopaedic mattresses. The internal height of each compartment is 70 cm – enough for sleeping – and a large window assures adequate ventilation.

Bizarrely, this moving hotel means that you probably travel less than if you were staying in a traditional hotel as you don't need to move around yourself to see different sites – you stay right at the sites themselves! Equally, your itinerary can span natural rather than national borders, say to see both Chilean and Argentinean Patagonia on the same trip. Trips through the Pantanal conservation area (the world's largest freshwater wetland) average around 800 km in a week; in Patagonia they drive 1,200 km in twelve days. The longest drives cover around 200 km a day, but still showcase the best of each region.

One of the other benefits of Exploranter is that you are much closer to the food, pcople and culture as you stay overnight in the local area rather than in the more sanitized surroundings of a regular hotel.

There is only one restriction – only foldable rucksacks are accepted on board. Hard bags are not allowed. You are therefore advised to pack light, using wisely the 80×32×35 cm locker provided for your belongings.

Exploranter
Rua Joaquim Antunes, 232
Escritório Central
São Paulo - Brazil
+55 (0)11 3085 2011
info@exploranter.com
www.exploranter.com
Twenty-seven single bunk rooms

Rates The price of trips varies significantly according to itinerary, however travellers should budget around US$ 90 per day to include transport, food and taxes for a trip. There is no supplement for single travellers and many guests come alone.

Location While the coach and trailer move, the office gives details of trips and schedules.

To do

The Exploranter provides an environment for people to meet each other, share adventures and enjoy new experiences. You don't have to be an adventurer, however you do need to be willing to get along with people. Guest ages range from 3 to 75 and the team balance individual freedom with group expeditions to create a real flavour of the region you're visiting.

Ariaú Amazon Towers

World's largest treehouse complex

First open in 1986, the Ariaú Amazon Towers offers amazing lodging in giant treehouses, linked by over 8 km of wooden catwalks 10 m above the forest floor and river delta below. Walking at night on these paths with the noises of the jungle around you is a truly amazing experience.

A steady stream of guests, celebrities and political leaders has already enjoyed this sprawling complex, which provides a memorable introduction to the Amazon.

Guest rooms are in one of the eight massive treehouses. The rooms are simply furnished but spacious and functional – especially considering their remote location. If possible choose a room with air conditioning (an additional US\$ 25 per night), as you'll see the benefit when humidity can be close to 95%. Check your room before accepting to make sure that it's appropriate for your needs. They have family bed combinations, queen beds and other variations. If you are considering a suite you might want to think about how much time you'll actually be spending in the room itself – mostly you'll be in the rainforest on tours or on the walkways themselves.

Pack ear plugs if you're a light sleeper. The complex is completely made from wood, so sound from your neighbours above, below and either side travels, and of course the noise of the rainforest starts at dawn. Resort dining offers themed buffet meals taken at set times that you eat with your provided group guide. The hotel also offers a couple of swimming pools and two 41 m observation towers providing a panoramic view., Mosquitoes are supposedly discouraged by the acidity of the river and don't pose a problem for guests. You should however take precautions as recommended by health agencies and personal requirements.

Ariaú Amazon Towers
rua Leonardo Malcher 699, Centro
CEP: 69010 170
Manaus – Amazonas - Brazil
+55 (92) 3245-1407
treetop@ariautowers.com.br
www.ariautowers.com
260 bedrooms

Rates
Ariaú Amazon Towers has 260 bedrooms, eleven suites, and nine "Tree Houses" or "Tarzan Suites" with prices ranging from US\$ 200-3,000, depending on package season and availability.
Note that there is a 10% service tax added to all package prices, extras and tours.

To do

All guests are on similar package tours that offer variations on piranha fishing, caiman watching and jungle tours, altering the number of nights and schedule of trips to allow different times to explore the walkways yourselves. If you can, allow half a day to visit the far reaches of the walkways or consider hiring bikes from the hotel. We recommend the dolphin excursions, which offer a chance to swim with flesh-coloured river dolphins (considered sacred in some cultures), without the mass-market pressure of trips advertised in destinations such as Florida. Manaus itself is a thriving industrial metropolis whose character was built upon rubber, yet still manages to demonstrate the enthusiasm that characterizes so much of Brazilian culture. As an international gateway it might be an alternative for entry into Brazil, as the immigration facilities are less busy than at other locations. Don't miss a night at the famous "jungle opera" if possible.

Location

The complex is located on the right bank of the Negro River, 60 km from Manaus, which is about 4 hours by air from Sao Paulo or Rio. It forms part of the National Park of the Negro River at the beginning of the Anavilhanas Archipelago, the largest freshwater archipelago in the world.
Shuttle buses pick up from Manaus hotels to take guests to the departure point at the riverside Tropical Hotel for boats to the resort. If you arrive early, there is a surprisingly nice zoo in the hotel grounds. The river cruise takes about 2 hours. Helicopter and fast boat transit are also available.

Elqui Domos

Million-star hotel dedicated to stargazing

The Chilean skies of the Elqui Valley are covered by cloud less than thirty days a year and are a regular destination for many of the world's astronomers. Enthusiast Esteban Zarate and his wife wanted somewhere peaceful to enjoy their hobby and chose the Elqui valley to build their unusual hotel. Using geodesic domes for simplicity and lightweight structure, they have created a stargazing platform from the comfort of your bed, with a detachable roof.

The dome tents have everything inside: a full bathroom, comfortable beds, heating, snack bar, etc., but you should still dress warmly. Night temperatures can drop to below freezing during winter nights (down to –10° C). However, cold air makes for clear skies, and the absence of light pollution in this remote location makes viewing conditions close to ideal.

The two-storey domes have a living room and bathroom on the ground floor. Upstairs is the main bed with detachable roof. Each dome also has a large terrace and you are provided with a quality telescope to use. You'll also find a stocked fridge, tea and coffee facilities as well as maps and magazines about astronomy.

Their on-site restaurant, Carinae (named after the most beautiful star you can see from the Southern Hemisphere) serves fusion food using local produce. Daylight provides an opportunity for picnics and barbecues by the river. All in all a very pleasant location!

For those unfamiliar with the night skies, Esteban and his team provide a stargazing tour and telescope-operating sessions to help you get the best from your evening viewings. They can also arrange a horseback stargazing tour, which should not be missed.

To do

Facilities for relaxation and entertaining partners less interested in the heavens are provided, with a swimming pool and spa with massage treatments available. Bikes can be hired if notified during booking and horse rides arranged for treks and tours through the beautiful valley scenery.

Elqui Domos
Camino Público Pisco Elqui Horcón km 3,5
Sector Los Nichos s/n
Paihuano - Región de Coquimbo - Chile
+ 56 2 1960474
reservas@elquidomos.cl
www.elquidomos.cl
Seven eco-domes for couples or cosy groups

Rates and location From 45,000 pesos (US$ 78) to 54,000 pesos (US$ 99) per dome per night based on double occupancy. Elqui Domos is about 1½ hours' drive (96 km / 60 miles) from the nearest large town of La Serena, on a road that is paved for all but the last 3 km (2 miles). Even this last stretch isn't difficult to drive at any time of year. You can even take a bus if you're feeling a little more adventurous.

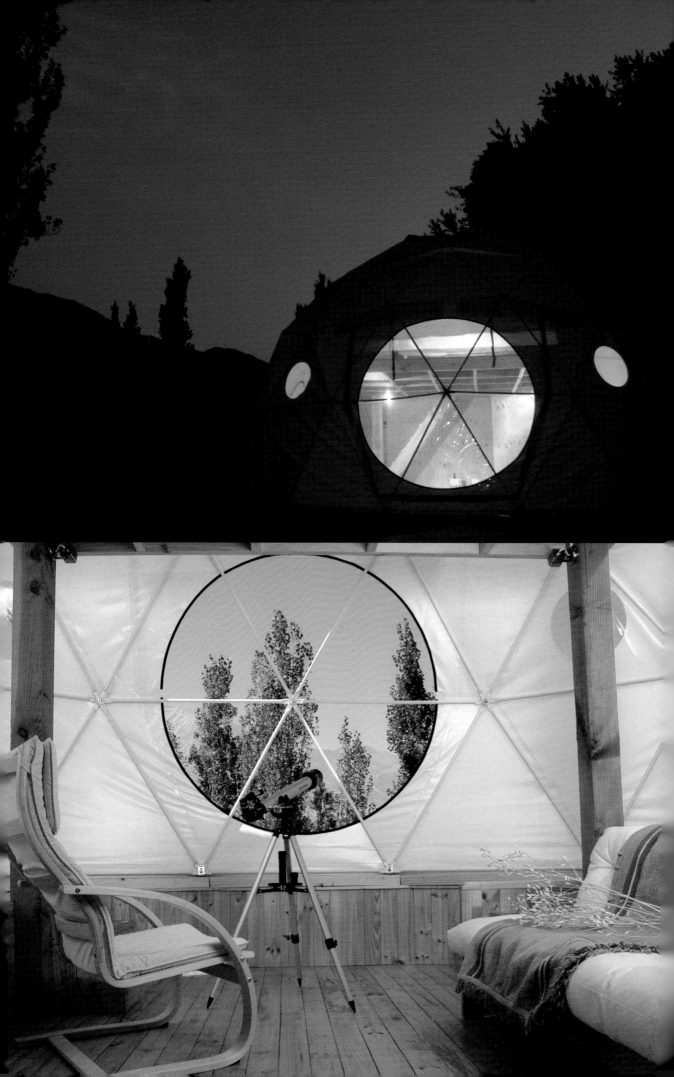

Magic Mountain Hotel

Forest accommodation in a fairytale mountain

Originally a place for friends to stay while they enjoyed the hunting and fishing resources of the Hulio Hulio reserve, the name is from a favourite book of the owners. The story describes a mountain that has magical powers and grants wishes – The Magic Mountain. With a waterfall cascading from the pinnacle of the roof, the lodge is indeed a special place. As you'd expect from staying somewhere remote, your senses become tuned to the vibrant ecosystem of the forest. Condors and eagles in the air, pumas on the ground. Waking with the dawn and enjoying nature.

Each of the thirteen rooms has a private bathroom. There are also eleven cabins, accommodating between four and six people. Rooms are named after plants and animals found in the park, although a little detective work with a good dictionary is required to try and translate some of the more obscure. "Lahuen" is a medical plant used by the local Mapuche Indians and "Ranita de Darwin" is a tiny frog close to extinction.

While you're some way from civilization, the lodge is self sufficient and has a restaurant "Meson del Bosque" (Forest Table). All meals are taken here and you'll get the opportunity to sample some really good Chilean cooking. When the weather is cold, try their pastel de papas – a mixture of mashed potatoes, onion, olives, egg and meat cooked in the oven. A recommendation for those with a sweet tooth is to try it with sugar, but beware! Too large a portion will leave you unable to do anything except snooze. Lighter fare includes the Chilean staple of cazuela – a meat or chicken soup with potatoes. Spice it up with merquen – the Mapuche's local red pepper.

During the evening the restaurant provides a bar where you can enjoy the traditional Chilean Pisco Sour. Made from grape liqueur mixed with lemon juice and sugar, it is particularly refreshing. Take care however, Pisco Sour is easy to drink and a hangover this far from a pharmacy is particularly painful if you've forgotten to pack aspirin.

Lodge Montaña Magica
Reserva de Huilo Huilo
Camino Internacional s/n km 60
Ruta TCH 203
Panguipulli - X Region - Chile
montanamagicalodge@gmail.com
www.huilohuilo.cl
Thirteen rooms in main building

Rates and location From US$ 110 to US$ 163 per person per room, based on a couple sharing including buffet breakfast. The lodge is 56 km (35 miles) from Panguipulli. The largest major city is Valdivia, around 130 km (80 miles) from the resort. Pichol airport is there and you should plan for a transfer of about 2 1/2 hours by car. The other airport is in Temuco, 140 km (85 miles) away – around 3 hours from Huilo Huilo.

To do

The lodge is located between two small villages, Puerto Fuy and Neltume, which grew up in the 1930s to support the logging industry. You can find small restaurants plus craft shops selling furniture and animal sculptures there. Neltume achieved fame in the 1970s and 1980s as the home of the revolutionary leader Commander Pepe. While reminders of the military campaigns still exist, the area is now more famous for fishing and hunting in summer and cross-country skiing on the volcano in winter. They have also constructed a 500 m (1,640 ft) aerial ropeway up to

90 m (300 ft) high in the forest canopy, allowing you to travel from tree to tree, over cliffs with traverses. The park also offers horse and mountain biking plus kayak trips on the Pirihueico Lake.

Climate is generally sunny with moderate temperatures, but the summer (December, January and February), can be very hot. The rainy season begins in April and finishes in October. Ski-lovers have better conditions in July and August while September to November and March to April are the best months for outdoor activities

Hotel Utter Inn

Sleep inside a floating aquarium, where the fish look in and you look out

For the ultimate seclusion for the night, consider sleeping in this underwater hotel in the middle of Lake Mälaren, 1 km (1/2 mile) from Västerås. Your room is reached by a water-taxi ride to a small hut on a floating steel platform moored a short distance from one of the outlying islands. There is a terrace with a couple of chairs. Inside, the giant steel hatch dominates the room and the rest of the space is taken up by a toilet (thankfully), cooker, small heater and some storage space. After a few brief instructions you're left to the solitude that artist Mikael Genberg originally intended the Utter (Otter) Inn to emphasize. Climb down the steps and your twin bedroom awaits, 3 m (10 ft) below the surface of the lake. Not a place for those scared of enclosed spaces, as once the hatch shuts you are very much in a different world, floating in an aquarium with four picture windows for the aquatic inhabitants to look in at you – and you to peek out.

Furnishings are simple (from IKEA of course). Two beds, a small table and a couple of low-voltage reading lights or a candle lantern for illumination.

A picnic dinner and breakfast are included in the deluxe package and after relaxing on the terrace chairs you retire below. It's eerily silent and as darkness finally falls you are gently rocked to sleep. The only noisy neighbours are the ones you choose to arrive with. Woken by the wake of an early-morning ferry shaking the hotel, you see a large pike that's been observing you as if window-shopping for a snack later on.

Pick your companion wisely as there is no escape from snoring in a steel box underwater!

Underwater hotel
Kopparbergsvägen 1, 721 87 Västerås
One cosy bedroom for two
Sweden
+46 (0)21 39 01 00
malarstaden@vasteras.se
www.vasterasmalarstaden.se

Rates and locations 1,500 kronor per person per night, including dinner and breakfast (US$220 / €165). The hotel opens at the beginning of April and the season runs through to late September. Your prearranged boat ride leaves from Västerås tourist port, about 40 minutes by train from central Stockholm, or 10 minutes by car from the low-cost airline gateway airport of Västerås.

To do

The less you bring with you, the more intense the feeling of isolation and solitude and the greater the experience. Some guests have the courage to swim around the platform, others prefer to stay dry, perhaps knowing that a hungry-looking pike lives in the lake. In summer, sunbathing would be an option. A small dinghy is provided should you wish to visit the nearby island, but all too soon the water taxi arrives to bring you back to the noise of the city. If you're still keen on something different after your stay underwater, check out Kolarbyn forest camp in Skinnskatteberg village, about an hour by car from Västerås. This forest location provides eco-lodge accommodation and even offers a moose safari during the summer. For further details see the relevant entry in this guide.

Hotel Hackspett

A self-contained treehouse in a city-centre location

13 m (42 ft) is a long way up any tree, let alone a 130-year-old oak in the central park of Västerås near Stockholm. The Hotel Hackspett (Woodpecker) is another extraordinary brainchild of Mikael Genberg, artist and innovator of this hotel and its sister, the underwater Utter (Otter) Inn on nearby Lake Mälaren.

Reached via a sturdy but wobbly rope ladder, the platform has an impressive view of the park below and out to the lake beyond. Advice to "pack light" was appreciated as your luggage is hoisted up on a rope from the treehouse platform.

On arrival you discover your picnic supper and breakfast packs waiting. There is the briefest of tours covering safety and operation of the most essential item at the top of a tree – a toilet. Pull up the rope ladder and you retire to find the treehouse well thought out and equipped. From an IKEA bed and duvet, heater and cooking facilities, Mikael has anticipated your needs. There are even a few books on a shelf and a small lantern to read by.

Surprisingly you never quite escape the background noise of the city centre, but the rustle of leaves and sound of children playing football below is rather calming. Your mind is at peace when you're sitting quietly in a tree, although not enough to appreciate birdsong from the crack of dawn. It's surprising how loud birds are when you're at their level!

At night, the only reminder of civilization is the faint roar of traffic on the road far below. If you really want peace and solitude however, don't forget to turn off your mobile phone – coverage is rather good from this treetop vantage point.

Kopparbergsvägen 1
721 87 Västerås,
Sweden
+46 (0)21 39 01 00
malarstaden@vasteras.se
www.vasterasmalarstaden.se
One cosy bedroom for two

Rates and location 1,500 kronor per person per night, including dinner and breakfast (US$220 / €165). The hotel opens at the beginning of April and the season runs through to late September. The treehouse is in the centre of Västerås city park, and most guests meet at the Västerås tourist office, about 40 minutes by train from central Stockholm, or 10 minutes by car from the low-cost airline gateway airport of Västerås.

To do

Västerås is a thriving town with restaurants and bars within a 5 minute walk of the park. Of course, you need to climb back up the rope ladder and so should take care if you're thinking of drinking – most guests climb up the tree and stay there until the following morning.

Just outside Västerås is the Vallby Friluftsmuseum – the largest open-air museum in Sweden. Old buildings such as a Viking farm and silversmith workshops have been recreated or moved here from all over the province. Don't forget that Västerås is also home to Kolarbyn forest cabins for moose watching and the famous Utter Inn underwater hotel, both covered in this guide.

Kolarbyn

*Sleep in a "camouflage" hut in the woods,
with no electricity*

Kolarbyn consists of twelve little forest huts located by the beautiful lake Skärsjön. Known as Sweden's most primitive hotel, the huts have no electricity and the dark evenings are lit by candles or traditional oil lamps. Each hut provides two berths with sheepskin rugs to cushion your slumber. You're kept warm by a wood heater, and your first task is to gather and chop enough wood for your cooking and heating needs.

During the week guests bring food to cook themselves at one of several fireplaces – one even has a view over the lake. The nearest supermarket is 3 km away at Skinnskatteberg, and pans and cutlery are available in the storehouse. At weekends, food can be provided for those making a reservation in advance.

There is also a sauna to chop wood for, although as washing facilities are limited to a stream, you are encouraged to be brave enough to cool down with a dip in the nearby lake.

Toilets are in natural outhouses which, though rustic, serve their purpose adequately, as was the normal practice for centuries!

Kolarbyn
Skinnskatteberg
Bergslagen
Sweden
+46 (0)73 40 6101
thomas@kolarbyn.se
www.kolarbyn.se

Rates Kolarbyn eco-lodge is open for individual guests from 1 May to 30 September. Rates for adults are 250 kronor per person (US$38 / €27), with children half price. Breakfast is 65 kronor (US$10 / €7) per person, with children 45 kronor (US$7 / €5). Prices for lodging include a sleeping mat, sheepskin rug, wood to cut for your fire, candles, matches, fresh water (to fetch yourself from the well) and access to fireplaces

for cooking. Kolarbyn recommend that you bring you own sleeping bag although they can be hired in advance for an additional 50 kronor (US$7 / €5) for your whole stay. You should also bring a torch and pillow.

Location Kolarbyn is a couple of hours by car from Stockholm and 45 minutes from Västerås. Trains run hourly from Stockholm Central Station to Köping, where there is a public bus connection to Skinnskatteberg for an arranged pick-up by the Kolarbyn team. Travel time is about 2 hours 20 minutes. Tickets may be purchased at train stations, on-line booking of train and bus tickets is cheaper.

To do

Providing a back-to-nature experience in the natural woods of Sweden, visitors can additionally book a number of guided excursions and even a romance package. Of particular note are the Moose Safari and Wolf Howling tours where you'll learn about the wild inhabitants of the forest in a practical way. Kolarbyn guides have been successful in finding wild moose on every moose safari for the past five years. As night falls the forest is brought to life and the animals awaken from their daytime slumber to feed. Through the identification of their hoof prints, fresh droppings and bite marks, plus knowledge of their favourite locations, the guides usually manage to find these kings of the Swedish forest. The night Wolf Howling tours are equally exciting, as a family of these near-extinct animals live close to Kolarbyn. While there are less than 200 wolves in the whole of Scandinavia, their numbers are slowly recovering and this tour provides the opportunity to understand more at first hand.

Ice hotel

Sleep at –5 °C in an ephemeral work of art

Although the Icehotel has become a classic of the unexpected and has featured in most of the world's magazines (Kate Moss and Naomi Campbell have been photographed here), it's still an undefinable place that will satisfy the most curious among you – and the least sensitive to the cold!

The peculiar feature of this hotel, first created in the early 1990s, is that it is (re)built every year at the beginning of winter with the frozen water of the nearby river, and it melts every spring. The cycle is complete: the river water turns to ice and then returns naturally to the river some six months later…

The Icehotel offers two types of accommodation: bedrooms or suites. In both cases you sleep on a block of ice covered with an insulating sheet and reindeer skins and the ambient temperature is around –5 °C. As the suites are all designed by different artists, if you have the means don't hesitate to book one of them, the impression of sleeping in an actual work of art is quite extraordinary.

The hotel also offers the famous and indispensable Icebar, open to non-residents, as well as an ice chapel sought out by some couples as a likely venue to get married…Although all this seems idyllic on paper, the sleeping bags are not always up to the task: if you want to avoid being wakened around 6 in the morning feeling cold, bring your own severe-weather sleeping bag… Also bring your warmest clothes, even if you'll probably wear the jumpsuit that the hotel kindly hands out to guests on arrival.

Finally, beware of the "warm rooms": they're comfortable but quite expensive and have no bathtub.

Of the two restaurants near the hotel, we strongly recommend the one furthest away: it is in a much more charming setting and the walk is very pleasant (see box on aurora borealis).

ICEHOTEL
981 91 Jukkasjärvi, Sweden
Tel.: +46 (0)980 668 00
E-mail: info@icehotel.com
www.icehotel.com
Around eighty rooms (number varies
from year to year)

Rates
From € 200 for a standard room and from € 300
for a suite

Location
A 30-minute drive from the town of Kiruna. If the
Stockholm-Kiruna flight is fully booked or too
expensive, you can take the direct-link night train.

See the aurora borealis

The aurora borealis phenomenon occurs frequently but isn't visible every day. So don't be disappointed if you happen to be there at a bad time. If the sky is clear, you'll need to go some distance from the hotel lights. A great idea is to walk to the second restaurant in the village, via the frozen lake. The walk (around 15 minutes) is magnificent at night when the conditions are optimal for seeing the northern lights.

Hitchhike to Kiruna in −35 °C

Despite what you might think, hitchhiking can be a good way of getting to Kiruna: cars pass fairly frequently and the cold, though intense (the outside temperature averages −35 °C...), is perfectly bearable for a few minutes if you're well wrapped up, as the air is very dry. Another plus is that you won't have to wait 20 minutes for a taxi at the hotel. Because of the climate, passing drivers rarely fail to stop...

Things to do

Whatever happens don't miss going out on a dog-sledging expedition. Allow at least two days to taste the magic of the polar nights. Mats Peterson is especially recommended: you'll drive your own sled pulled by four dogs and sleep at his place, in an insulated wooden cabin in the middle of nowhere. Mats is an experienced sledger: he was even chosen to organize an outing for the king and queen of Sweden. At Kiruna, visits to the iron-ore mine and the wooden church, a Swedish national monument, are irresistible. http://kiruna.se/ (click on "Tourism" then "Dogsledging")

Hotel Kakslauttanen

Unique glass igloos to see the Aurora Borealis in comfort

In order to marvel at the amazing Northern Lights, Hotel Kakslauttanen provides a choice of futuristic glass igloos as well as traditional snow igloo and wood cabin accommodation. While snow igloos are a winter speciality, the glass igloos are available all year round. The first five glass igloos were opened in 2004 and such was guest feedback that a further fifteen were built in 2006.

Using temperature-resistant glass, these igloos keep the inside warm, while the outside is –30 °C. This allows you to lie in bed and, if you're lucky, see the amazing Aurora Borealis lightshow. This natural phenomenon usually appears in the night sky between the end of August and April, however peak activity is around April and September.

For more traditional winter fun, Hotel Kakslauttanen offers log cabins all year round and snow igloos from late December to April. As with all snow and ice hotel accommodation, the interior is cool, typically between –3 °C and –6 °C, and you'll need the warm sleeping bag provided so you don't feel the cold.

Hotel Kakslauttanen
Twenty each of snow and glass igloos
FI-99830 Saariselkä
Lapland · Finland
+358 (0)16 667 100
hotel@kakslauttanen.fi · www.kakslauttanen.fi
Thirty two log cabins, twenty snow igloos
and twenty glass igloos

Rates Snow igloos on a half-board basis are from €200 per person per night, or around €312 for a couple sharing. Glass igloos on a couple-sharing basis are around €368 half board for two. There are discounts for children and longer stays and special programme prices apply for Christmas and the New Year.

To do

Many guests arriving in Kaamos – "polar night" or the time between December and January when the sun doesn't rise – describe the experience as mystical, because the snow reflections create a virtual twilight / dawn effect all the time. Of course, you need to plan the time of year to visit according to what you want to experience. The Laplanders have plenty to keep you occupied all year round, although the winter activities are most famous, from husky, reindeer or snowmobile safaris to ice fishing. They even run a course for you to try your hand at snow carving. The hotel boasts the largest smoke sauna in the world, which has to be tried. Although many try the traditional cool-down of rolling naked in the snow – only a few are brave enough to try the most extreme cool-down of all, swimming in a hole cut in the ice.

Location
The closest airport is Ivalo Airport, about 40 km
(25 miles) away. The hotel can arrange car or
snowmobile transfers. For reference, Helsinki is
1,085 km (674 miles) away and the nearest ATM is
in Saariselka village, 10 km (6 miles) away.

Pavilion Hotel

Rock'n'roll chic in this inspired art hotel

Sourcing fabrics, wallpaper, room fixtures and fittings from around the world, Danny and his sister Noshi converted a once-neglected London town-house hotel into an artistic and funky place to hang out. From minimalist decor in some rooms, to funky 70s, their thirty rooms cater for a variety of tastes. Rooms are eccentrically crammed with delicate artefacts that in some cases have not stood up to the relentless wear of guests and souvenir hunters. Although equipped with TV / DVD combos, don't expect the rooms to be large and be prepared for small but functional en suite facilities.

Bathroom facilities are not why people stay here, nor is the continental breakfast left on a tray outside your room and Danny informs guests that a "full English" is available in the dining room of the adjoining hotel for an additional charge, if requested in advance. If you're fussy about this kind of detail then this hotel isn't for you. For the great majority, the rooms have more than enough charm to satisfy guests. The sizes and styles vary, from the tiny "Quiet Please" single room, to the opulence of "White Days Soul Nights".

Everyone has their favourites – from those that you want to sleep in yourselves, such as the four-poster of "Indian Summer", to those that you just want to tell your friends about – such as the mirror beads and 70s' disco fever glitter-ball look of "Honky Tonk Afro".

Both Noshi and Danny are friendly hosts and they have built a great reputation with stars from the TV and music industry keen to sample somewhere with character at very affordable prices. Bryan Ferry, Duran Duran and other 80s heyday artists still call the Pavilion home when playing in London, as does regular guest Courtney Pine. Kate Moss and Pete Doherty were one-time regular guests, although Pete is now banned after hosting a particularly memorable and niche gig in his bedroom.

The Pavilion has a really sensible 12 noon checkout, so that fun-seekers can enjoy a lie-in after a late night in London.

Pavilion Hotel
34–36 Sussex Gardens, Hyde Park,
London W2, UK
+44 (0)207 262 0905
info@pavilionhoteluk.com
www.pavilionhoteluk.com
Thirty en suite bedrooms

Rates and location There are 30 rooms. Single are from £60 to £85 and doubles and twins £100. Family rooms are £130. Prices are per room per night and inclusive of continental breakfast and taxes. A 5 minute walk from Edgware Road underground station on the Circle or District lines and a 10 minute taxi ride from mainline stations. 20 minutes on foot to Hyde Park and the Oxford Street shops.

To do

London needs no introduction,
and the hotel is close to tube and mainline
railway stations. There is a thriving
Lebanese community on Edgware Road
a few minutes' walk from the hotel.
You'll find falafel restaurants and bars
all the way down this busy street, with
patrons sitting outside smoking sheesha.
How the July 2007 public smoking ban
will affect these places is unknown –
probably very little as they aren't known
for their strict observance of legality.
However, if you enjoy ethnic or Moroccan
cuisine, rather than these undoubtedly
authentic eateries, you might do well to
take a 10 minute taxi ride to Momo on
Heddon Street, for an equally good and
more relaxed meal – in a quiet backstreet
off Oxford Circus and Regent Street

The Old Railway Station

Pullman carriage luxury accommodation

Providing four suites in restored Orient Express Pullman carriages as well as rooms in the original station house, The Old Railway Station is a landmark of rail-lover accommodation.

Luxury train journeys were once defined by the Orient Express with their Pullman carriages and two examples have been lovingly restored here. Some elements have been improved – they now have working central heating, while others have simply been retained – such as the splendour of the decorations.

It is not impossible to imagine yourself returning to the heyday of steam and The Old Railway Station provides a perfect overnight stop if you're planning to participate in nearby themed events such as the historic Goodwood Revival motorsport weekend. Anniversaries would have a touch of class here, especially if you choose to do the right thing and dress appropriately for the occasion, as would have been required in a Pullman.

The Old Railway Station
Petworth, West Sussex GU28 0JF - UK
+44 (0)1798 342 346 - info@old-station.co.uk
www.old-station.co.uk
Four railway carriage suites

Rates and location There are four railway carriage suites and midweek breaks are from £97 per room to £168. The station house offers rooms from £84. There is a minimum two-night stay during weekends and it is worth checking availability for midweek package offers. Petworth is 16 km (10 miles) from Midhurst on the South Downs, around 45 minutes by car from Gatwick airport.

Harlingen Lighthouse

Sleep overlooking the town in this lighthouse tower

Sister property to the Dockside Crane hotel, Harlingen Lighthouse is not difficult to find – it's in the heart of the historic docks, towering above the surrounding houses. Look for an Art Deco beacon. Unlike many lighthouses it has no need to be remote, as it protected navigation from the sandbanks around the port itself.

After climbing the eighty or so steps, you uncover a three-storey luxury haven, providing all-round panoramic views from your bedroom and upstairs lookout, with added facilities including TV, tuner/CD unit, minibar and a hot-drinks facility. The bedroom is beautifully equipped, not surprisingly with a hand-made (and comfortable) bed. One floor below the bedroom is the bathroom with a giant shower and facilities. Thankfully, the designers have ensured that the nautical theme is retained and the original lantern room at the top provides a VHF radio so you can hear the movements of shipping traffic, as well as wind speed and direction meters. The outside balcony can also be accessed, should you wish to brave the elements yourself.

Looking down on the city and docks below is endlessly fascinating – and looking down on the birds flying even more so. Binoculars are provided!

Inside is surprisingly spacious, however some of the steps and ladders are steep – so pack your belongings in a soft bag, and travel light.

Harlingen Lighthouse formed part of a network of lights along the Dutch coast. Eighteen of the twenty lighthouses are still in use. The other disused lighthouse, in the Hook of Holland, is now a museum.

Havenweg 1
Harlingen Lighthouse,
The Netherlands
+36 (0)517 414410
www.vuurtoren-harlingen.nl
One double suite

Rates
The double room costs €279 for a couple sharing for 2007 including tax (€319 for bookings in 2008). Breakfast is included in the price, delivered to the bottom of the lighthouse steps by the friendly hostess team. The team don't accept online reservations as they prefer to assist you by phone. Reception is mainly open in the morning, but first

check their website for any additional questions. Expect to book far in advance or be flexible with your dates as this hotel is extremely popular with honeymoon couples and for anniversaries.

Location
The lighthouse is next to the Harlingen Dokkade (docks) station, close to the city centre of Harlingen, only 10 minutes' walk from the shops and restaurants of this thriving Dutch seaside town.

First built: 1920–1922, Architect: C. Jelsma
Restored: 1998–1999, Architect: B. Pietersma
Position: 53 10' 09" NL; 05 25' 04" EL
Highest lookout point: 24 m (80 ft) above average floodwater

To do

Harlingen is also host to crane and lifeboat hotels, which you should check out for a future visit. The town itself is pleasant and you'll be lucky to get a night in the crane and lighthouse on the same weekend. The lighthouse is particularly popular, booked over a year in advance to honeymoon and anniversary couples. Get in while you can, a night is worth the trip! Shops and bars are close by and there are plenty of international and local restaurants in the town.

Dockside Crane

Rotate your private industrial crane

The second of three unusual hotels in Harlingen, this amazing converted dockside crane has been the recipient of intelligent engineering and dedicated devotion rarely seen in a private home – let alone in a hotel property. Replacing the old external ladders with modern lifts to gain entry, the old machine room in the body of the crane has been transformed into a luxurious bedroom that wouldn't be out of place in the most modern of designer hotels.

Managers Willem and Carla have kept the existing observation windows and industrial feel, but have added comfort, warmth and the latest flat screen and audio equipment to create a fantastic environment to enjoy a childhood dream for many – your own personal, WORKING crane. Even though they've fitted a luxury double shower and designer toilet, the crane can still swirl around controlled from the comfort of the driver's cabin.

A fantastic breakfast of fresh local pastries, eggs and a deli selection is included, delivered magically via the internal lift to your bedroom. Entry to the crane itself is effortless as lifts are provided to the main bedroom area. The top picnic area and crane cabin are accessed via a ladder from the main bedroom, but you rarely feel enclosed or uncomfortable about the height. This is a solid, trustworthy block of metal, and even when rotating you recognize that it's capable of lifting tons of goods, so you and your bedroom don't pose a problem.

Arrive promptly, and take advantage of the panorama, as rain or shine this is a spectacular vantage point from which to view the old docks. With a crane at your disposal, you're sure to find yourself spinning the platform instead of watching the DVDs supplied.

Following booking acceptance and payment, the Harlingen crane team will send you a comprehensive arrival pack. Even though the lifts allow entry for even the most vertigo-challenged and fitness-free, pack your belongings in a squashy bag, as one of the lifts is small and will only accept a small bag and you at the same time.

Dokkade 5
Harlingen,
The Netherlands
+36 (0) 517 414410
www.vuurtoren-harlingen.nl

Rates The double room costs €299 for a couple sharing for 2007 including tax, (€319 for bookings in 2008). Breakfast is included in the price, delivered unseen into your room by the magic column lift. As with the other Harlingen entries, the team don't accept online reservations. Reception is mainly open in the morning, but first check their website for any additional questions first.

lifeboat hotels, which you should check out for a future visit to the town. Shops and bars are close by and there are plenty of international and local restaurants in the town. While Harlingen isn't perhaps a destination in its own right, a stay in any of the three unusual properties here is worthwhile. Since you're only an hour from Amsterdam, and close to the Controversy Tram hotel at Hoogwoud, if you don't mind moving hotel every day or so, these hotels alone would justify a trip.

Harlingen Lifeboat
A converted lifeboat still providing shelter after fifty years' service

The third of the trio of unusual hotels in Harlingen is the Lilla Marras lifeboat which provided sanctuary during 105 daring sea rescues between 1955 and 1979 along the English coast, saving forty-five lives. Now converted to luxury accommodation, it still offers sanctuary – but only from the stresses of daily life. The traditional lines of an ocean workhorse would suggest a sparse interior, however intelligent design and professional craftsmanship have created an overnight home equal to the most luxurious designer properties. Restored by the same Harlingen team that brought Harlingen harbour crane and lighthouse back to life, the Lilla Marras is indeed a work of art. While everything has been done to make

to a beautiful mahogany bath, this is still an ocean-going vessel that may be taken out to sea for those hiring a private captain for a couple of hours. Even though you're moored next to the city centre, you're in a quiet part of the historic docks, and there is little noise to disturb you from your slumbers, save for the gentle rocking of the boat itself. Breakfast of freshly baked bread (still warm from the bakers), boiled eggs and a continental cheese and ham selection is delivered by unseen housekeepers to the pilot cabin upstairs. It can be enthusiastically enjoyed on deck, or in the comfort of the aft cabin which provides day-time space. While you don't need to be overly athletic to enjoy the lifeboat, there is an element of bending and balance in staying here. While lovingly restored to a luxurious standard, it's still a lifeboat.

Location
Close to the city centre of Harlingen, you're only a
10 minutes walk from the shops and restaurants of
this thriving Dutch seaside town, and about 2 minutes
from the Dokkade railway station. Harlingen is
a working dockside town, but you're in the quiet
historic port, next to the harbour- master's office
and historic square -rigger boats.

Controversy *Tram Hotel*

Sleep in a tram or a train

In a remote corner of the Netherlands, crazy and friendly owners Frank and Irma Appel have created themed tram bedrooms in either end of two city-centre tram railcars that used to run on the streets of Amsterdam and in Germany. They've also converted a railway carriage into a luxurious double room, complete with a jacuzzi in the shape of a giant Mexican sombrero. The trams have double beds, shower and toilet facilities as well as a sink-top unit for drinks and snacks. They are arranged into four themed compartments: Italian (smoking), French (smoking), English (non-smoking) or American (non-smoking). A library with books, comics and old videos is provided for tram and rail carriage guests to while away a lazy afternoon. Painted silver, it looks like a spaceship – but is actually the escape pod from an oil rig, floating on a mini lake all its own.

Next to the trams and railway carriage is the Appel house, "Controversy" – named after their love of the similarly titled Prince album. You can't help but appreciate the lifestyle that Frank and Irma have created. They sleep inside a London double-decker bus installed in the living room, their kitchen and breakfast area is a converted French van and their house is decorated with cars and motor paraphernalia. A Cadillac and an amazing trike made from a Mercedes car in your lounge? A Lamborghini next to your bedroom? It's all at the Appel house.

There isn't a full restaurant on site, but Irma provides a wide breakfast selection from the main house and is always on hand with helpful advice.

Outside in the grounds, a MiG fighter plane is perched on top of a road roller – providing a surreal landmark for the property to help it stand out from the surrounding flat land around Hoogwoud.

Konongspade 36,
1718 MP Hoogwoud
The Netherlands
+36 (0)226 352693
info@controversy.nl
www.controversy.nl
Five double rooms

Rates The five rooms cost from €60 per person per night, including a great breakfast, tour of the amazing Appel home, tourist tax and cleaning. If you plan to stay for several nights, the rate reduces on the second night to €50 per person per night and the third night or more only €40 per person per night.

To do
There isn't much locally for tourists in Hoogwoud, which is a working farming community. However, you're close to both the coast and Amsterdam

Location A local map will help you find Hoogwoud, which is off the main road between Amsterdam and Harlingen. Once you're within range, it's easy to see Controversy – there aren't many places with trams, trains and fighter planes in their garden. If you're arriving by train and planning to stay several nights, ask Irma if she can pick you up – or arrange a taxi from the local station.

To do

Bikes with locks are provided for the luxury and survival-plus packages, which are useful for touring the city. The Hague is home of the Netherlands parliament and there are a number of official buildings, art galleries and museums to visit. A recommendation to consider is the Escher in Het Paleis (Escher in the Palace) museum (www.escherinhetpaleis.nl), based around the work of Dutch artist

M. C. Escher, who was famous for his lithographs of everyday objects twisted into surreal landscapes and incredibly complex geometric illusions. His work is appreciated by all kinds of people for both artistic quality and technical genius. This museum pays homage to Escher's art including an interactive exhibit where you walk through some of his work in virtual reality.

Capsule Hotel

Escape overnight in your own survival pod

Moored in The Hague, your room is a bright orange survival pod which once saw service on an oil rig platform. Originally built in 1972, they are 4.25 m (14 ft) in diameter and unaltered apart from the addition of a lock on the outside and an "emergency" chemical toilet inside. While not everyone's luxury choice, each pod provides cosy protection from the elements for up to three occupants.

First created for accommodation as an art project in 2004, owner Denis Oudendijk has eight different models ready for use and is currently working on additional locations in central Amsterdam and Nantes, France.

A number of overnight packages are available from a basic survival package with a sleeping bag and emergency rations, through to a James Bond themed luxury offering. This package has to be tried (think of the final escape pod scene of From Russia with Love), for its kitsch factor of a disco mirror ball, fairy-light decorations and sleeping bags with silk liners replacing the basic cotton. To get you in the correct mood, the luxury package also includes a DVD player with all the Bond movies on disc. In addition, your survival box is transformed into a luxury version with goodies including sparkling wine and a collection of vodka bar miniatures to create your own Martinis, shaken or stirred!

Whatever your choice of package, the bathroom facilities are non-existent / basic, with baby-wipe towels and bottled water to replace traditional shower and toilet facilities.

Capsule Hotel
Verheeskade 287, 2521DE,
Den Haag
The Netherlands
No tel. • denis@vlnr.info
www.capsulehotel.info
Two pods

Rates and location The luxury package costs €150 per capsule, while the survival-plus and survival offerings cost €100 and €70 respectively, inclusive of taxes. Discounts for students. All capsules can be booked up to a month ahead and a deposit of 10% is required to confirm your reservation. The pods are moored in a quiet area of the water, but rock a little when you're inside. While the bars of The Hague are appealing, a little caution is advised as you need dexterity and a firm grip to enter and don't really want to risk falling into the docks.

Euromast TV Tower

Two luxury rooms on top of a TV tower

The Euromast tower is a feature of the skyline of Rotterdam, and has been a regular tourist attraction since it was built in the 1960s. Already known as a great brunch venue, there are also two suites available for advance booking – "Heaven" and "Stars", perched 100 m (over 300 ft) above the city.

After the crowds have gone, suite occupiers are left to the night skyline in luxury with polished wooden floors, comfortable double beds, minibar and room service through to 1 am. For night owls, reception is open 24 hours. With the amazing view below, the wireless internet is perhaps unnecessary, although mobile phone coverage is very poor (if not non-existent). The larger of the two suites, "Heaven", has a great view of the docks and can provide a child's cot (at additional charge). It also has a great shower and designer black toilet tissue. The smaller suite, "Stars", looks over the Rotterdam city skyline, and has a bathroom jacuzzi.

Balcony access is from 10 pm until 10 am, so you have plenty of time to enjoy the cool night air and really enjoy the view of city and docks far below. We were warned that in winter, the rooms can be a little cold (they have big windows, but are only single glazed), but more worrying perhaps is that not only are you able to look out – the occupants of the other suite can look in from the shared balcony … so consider closing the curtains if your nightwear isn't suitable for external viewing …

Euromast, Parkhaven 20
3016 GM Rotterdam
The Netherlands
+36 (0) 10 24 1 1 7 88
suites@euromast.nl
www.euromast.nl
Two double suites

Rates
Both suites are €385.00 per night including an extensive breakfast (in your suite or at the brasserie at the top of the tower).

To do

You're a short taxi ride from
the centre of Rotterdam, with restaurants,
bars and nightlife, so aren't short on
there's no shortage of things to do.
Take one of the yellow water taxis
for a tour to see the docks, or just to try
a different way of getting about.

Location

Euromast is in the Parkhaven, but consider the parking restrictions if you arriveing by private car, orotherwise consider takinge a taxi. While parking carnets are available from the tower shop, it can prove expensive if you leave your car for the day, and you'll need to perhaps feed the meter again when you'd rather be tucked up in bed enjoying your breakfast.

Kruisherenhotel

Sleep in a 15th-century monastery

Serving originally as a monastery and church for the Order of Kruisheren (Crutched Friar) since 1438, this building fell into disrepair in the 1980s. The transformation into a luxurious, contemporary designer hotel was undertaken by Camille Oostwegel, who commenced large-scale renovation in late 2000. The character of the original monastery has been maintained in this complex project as, although designer furnishings and modern amenities have been provided in the rooms, they contrast with the stained-glass windows, Gothic vaulted ceilings and elegant stonework of the original building. Antiquity and modern design have been interwoven throughout. A mezzanine area has been created in the former nave of the church to provide a breakfast area with views of the town through the large windows of the former chancel. The nave also houses reception and the hotel lobby, plus a wine bar for "spiritual" refreshment. Side chapels are converted to lounge areas and the spacious stone corridors give a feeling of quiet reflection.

The bedrooms are housed in the former cloisters behind traditional solid oak doors that block unwanted noise from any guests unaware of how well sound travels along these stone corridors. Comfortably furnished, the rooms have wooden floors and quality designer fittings. Wall hangings, photographs and paintings tell stories of legends such as that of Saint Gertrude, patron saint of travellers, and it's obvious that a lot of thought has gone into the restoration to retain the "monastery mood".

Kruisherenhotel Maastricht
Kruisherengang 19-23
NL 6211 NW Maastricht
The Netherlands
+31 (0)43 329 20 20
info@kruisherenhotel.com
www.chateauhotels.nl
Fifty rooms and suites in former cloisters

Rates and location Fifty of the sixty rooms are in the cloisters, with the others in the gatekeeper's lodge or new building. We recommend confirming which you require when booking. From €150 (US$210) per person per night, based on a couple sharing.
The hotel is in the centre of Maastricht, on the restored Kommelplein square, about 5 minutes' walk from the more famous Vrijthof square.

To do

Maastricht has all the trappings of a busy city with shops, boutiques and café terraces. There are plenty of historic buildings as well as more modern architecture such as the new Hoge Brug (High Bridge), which crosses the River Meuse to the modern Céramique district. Check out the Bonnefanten museum here or perhaps visit the Maastricht caves. Tours often highlight a boat ride as part of the attraction, but you should be aware that this only lasts about 15 minutes, so don't expect too much time afloat. Tours run in various languages at different times of the day, so if you're planning to go to learn the interesting history of the caves, check with the hotel for the times of the appropriate language.

Propeller *Island City Lodge*

*Outrageous bedroom designs from upside-down
to inside a coffin*

From an upside-down room with a bed on the ceiling, to coffin and prison-cell rooms, this is no ordinary designer hotel. Originally created to pay for the musical interests of artist Lars Stroschen, the hotel grew from a couple of rented rooms to today's thirty-one individually designed rooms.

Some rooms are minimalist in their decoration – "Therapy" is completely white, with a variety of room colouring made possible using a series of coloured lights. The big mirror above the bed allows you to literally see yourself in a different light.

Other rooms offer an increasingly surreal experience, with the "Gruft / Coffin" offering a pair of coffins for beds, and "Freedom" a recreation of a prison cell, complete with escape through the wall. "Upside-Down" has a bed, table and furnishings suspended from the ceiling – and you sleep by opening a loft hatch in the floor. Not recommended after a night enjoying the many bars of Berlin!

The "Mirror" room completely surrounds you with mirrors as you'd expect, but taken to such extremes that it provides a kaleidoscope experience from every angle. Some rooms demonstrate the sense of humour of the artist, such as "Space-Cube" where a divider can be lowered to turn the double bed into two singles, perhaps after a late-night argument! Equally bizarre is the "Padded Cell".

Lars has not only built the rooms but the team that support guests from scratch – and everywhere you look you can see a creative genius at work. While there is no restaurant, you're in central Berlin so won't struggle to find a choice of food.

Once you've tried one room, you'll want to sample them all.

To do

Consider the Berlin Underground tours running all year round (Friday – Monday) to visit the underground sights of this once divided city. From Second World War WWII bunkers, to Cold War installations and factories, plus a pneumatic postal system and the city sewers. Tickets and details are available from the Main Office of Berliner Unterwelten, located in the southern entrance of the U8 subway station Gesundbrunnen.

Propeller Island City Lodge
Allbrecht Achilles Strasse 58
10709 Berlin
Germany
+49 (0)30 891 9016
www.propellerisland.de
Thirty-one outrageous rooms

Rates From €69 to €190 per night.
Breakfast is €7 per person.

Location You're 25 minutes by bus from the central Tegel airport, or 45 minutes from the larger Schonefeld. The nearest U-Bahn stop is Adenauer Platz, a 10 minute walk from the hotel.

Künstlerheim Luise

Co-operative art gallery where you can spend the night

Guests walking into a room at the Künstlerheim Luise art hotel find themselves within a work of art where every one of the fifty rooms is unique – even more so when you appreciate the partnership that the hotel makes with the artists who have decorated every room. A percentage of the profit from the individually created rooms is provided as payment – plus a number of free overnight stays. So while the art is stunning the rooms remain functional and all rooms and suites have a shower or bath, TV and free wireless internet.

The building itself is a residential palace dating from 1825, which like so many old properties in the former GDR had fallen into disrepair. The efforts of an enterprising group of young artists in 1984 transformed the property from a dilapidated art studio into a boutique hotel. In 2003 an annex was added to enclose the courtyard. This addition, as well as overall refurbishment and fitting of double glazing, has at last blocked the noise of the nearby elevated S-Bahn. Previously, earplugs were a necessary addition to guests' nightwear. While the classical style of the main building has been maintained, the new addition is more in tune with urban art, using exposed concrete, steel and glass. This serves to highlight the artistic nature of the different rooms and provides a gallery space for regular exhibitions next to the lobby.

As well as rooms and gallery space there is a restaurant, "Habel", named after the old vintner of Frederick the Great, and founder of the Berlin winery Gebrüder Habel in 1779.

Arte Luise Kunsthotel
Luisenstrasse 19,
10117 Berlin
Germany
+49 (0)30 28448 0
info@luise-berlin.com
www.luise-berlin.com
Fifty en suite rooms

Rates and location Doubles from €121–150 per room per night according to season and availability, inclusive of local sales taxes.
The Arte Luise is situated in the heart of this vibrant city, close by the Tiergarten park and Spree River, within view of the Reichstag building, Friedrichstrasse, Unter den Linden and the Brandenburg Gate.

To do

In summer we recommend hiring a bike for a tour through the centre of Berlin or along the River Spree. They can be delivered to the hotel for a daily fee of around €12. For those less energetic, most city bus tours of Berlin start at Brandenburger Tor, around the corner from the hotel. Also worth checking out is the Scheunenviertel area, centred on Oranienburger Strasse and Hackescher Markt for hip restaurants in the side streets as well as boutique and designer shopping. See the Propeller Island entry in this guide for alternative activities to consider in Berlin.

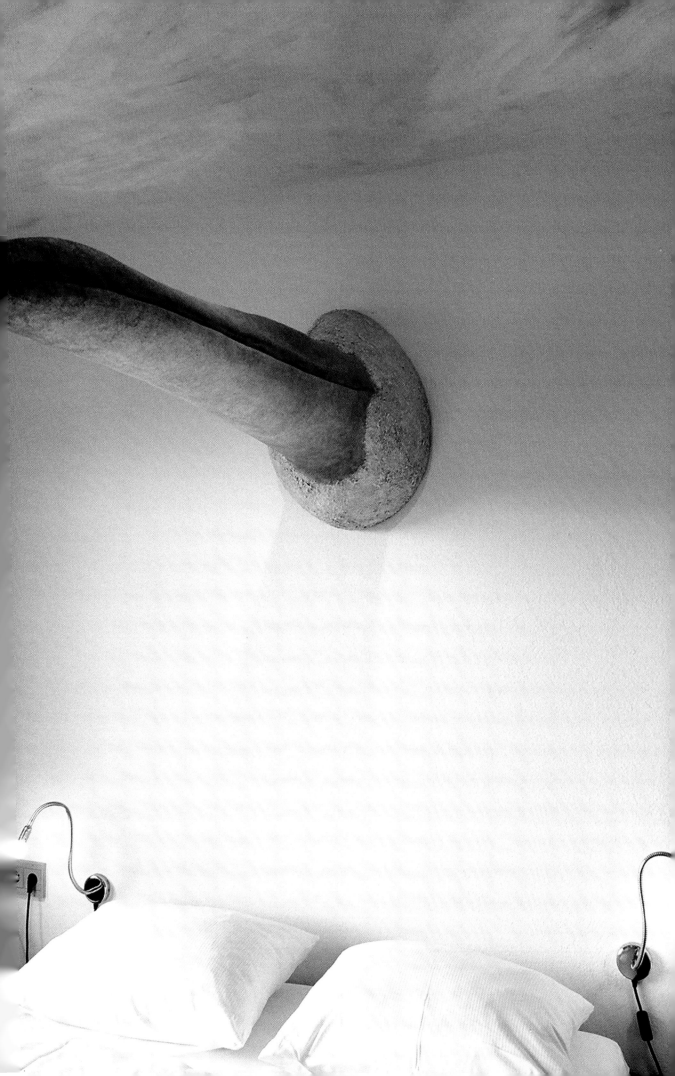

Baumhaus Hotel

First treehouse hotel to open in Germany

First opened in June 2005, it is arguable whether this is the first treehouse hotel in Germany or the craziest. Whatever the decision, these two-storey dwellings are furnished in a rustic style, with brightly coloured walls and off-angle windows, and are sure to entertain.

Each treehouse contains an "emergency toilet", but if only for the sake of the cleaners, a central toilet block is provided on one of the lower decks, with running water. The central area also contains a particularly German addition – a mini-bar filled with beer ready for evening guest celebrations. Treehouses additionally share an extraordinary open-air, chilled-water shower with a metal grid floor, so you can see the ground below you. Whether this is for health reasons, for waking up, or perhaps because of the provision of the guest mini-bar, sobering up is unknown.

Some treehouses have small balconies and each is themed according to the regional tradition and myths of trolls and fairy folk. Electric heating is provided for those brave enough to extend the summer open season into November and risk snow. A breakfast buffet is served in the main site restaurant.

Baumhaus Hotel
Fa. Künstlerische Holzgestaltung
Jürgen Bergmann
02829 Neisseaue OT Zentendorf
Görlitz - Germany
+49 (0)35891 491 0 • Info@kulturinsel.de
www.kulturinsel.de
Five treehouses for up to four guests each

Rates and location From €180 to €220 for up to four people, including breakfast and tax. Check out their last-minute deals as well, which offer up to 27% discounts for bookings with less than four days' notice. By car, leave the A4 (Dresden-Bautzen-Görlitz) autobahn at Görlitz, towards Rothenburg. Around 2 km (1 mile) from Zentendorf you'll see signs to the site.

Rogner Bad Blumau

Spa hotel designed by eccentric Austrian artist Hundertwasser, with grass-covered roofs and rainbow façades

Spa hotel designed by eccentric Austrian artist Friedenreich Hundertwasser, with grass-covered roofs and rainbow façades

Inaugurated in 2000, Rogner Bad Blumau has a simply amazing eclectic design with the roof of the main buildings grass-covered, following the profile of the rolling hills.

Some of the rooms are underground, with windows facing lit court-yards, while others follow the rolling landscape. A spa is at the centre of the complex, with an award-winning gourmet restaurant among the facilities. The spa has a variety of saunas and health facilities and offers a number of wellness programmes. The hot springs also provide heat and generate power for the resort.

Although the rooms are in differently themed areas, they provide a similar level of guest comfort, room service and en suite facilities. Inside, you could easily be in a well furnished four-star hotel. Outside, however, the story is dramatically different and the views are more in keeping with how you expect a hotel will look on the moon, or in a fantasy world – such is the patchwork of coloured tiles, grass and oddly positioned windows in the overall design.

Hundertwasser's artistic vision shares common themes, bright colours, organic forms, strong individualism, and a rejection of the straight line. Calling straight lines "the devil's tools", his architectural work is comparable to Antoni Gaudí. His work has been used for flags, stamps, coins, posters, schools, churches and, most impressively, a public toilet in his adopted home of New Zealand: no matter where he went in the world, his watch was always set to New Zealand time.

To do

Visit the Zotter Chocolate factory and Chocolate Theatre in Riegersburgabout, 30 km (18 miles) south-west of Bad Blumau. You are taken on a glass-covered path through the factory, restored in 2007, and invited to try products at tasting stations along the production line. The tour ends with near-unlimited nibbles including chocolate with chilli or ginger and around 100 other organic, Fairtrade combinations.

Rogner Bad Blumau
A 8283 Bad Blumau 100
Austria
+43 (0)3383 5100-0
spa.blumau@rogner.com
www.blumau.com
312 designer rooms including eight underground "Forest" houses and thirteen "Eyelid" apartments

Rates
Double room prices vary according to season and are from €120 per person per night plus tax, including unlimited use of the spa pool facilities. Suites are additionally available from €260 per night with spa treatment packages available on request.

Location
The hotel is around 56 km (35 miles) from Graz airport
and 1 km (1/2 mile) from Bad Blumau railway station
for visitors travelling by train.

Das Park Hotel

Sleep in a concrete pipe

Although Das Park is a one-off hotel, it has been designed from the outset to use worldwide standard concrete drainage or sewage pipe sections – so you could well see more of them in the future.

The idea of Andreas Strauss, the first rooms were built after the idea received sponsorship from the concrete tube manufacturer. The beauty of these pipes is that the utilitarian look needs little alteration to make them habitable – a coat of varnish is all that's necessary. The tubes have also had wall paintings by the Austrian artist Thomas Latzel Ochoa to make them seem a little more user-friendly. After a season or two, they can even be returned to the manufacturer for reuse, as the bed, door and lock mechanism, as well as the lighting and internet access are all easy to remove. Like cave hotels, Das Park Hotel is cool in the summer, and perhaps still warm in winter, although at the moment the hotel is only open from May to October.

Each tube weighs 9 ½ tons – so although some people might be tempted to rock or vandalize them, they are incredibly robust and need little maintenance. You do however need a hefty crane to lift them into place.

Rooms are accessed by a digital lock, whose code is provided by the self-service website upon booking acceptance. Once inside, facilities are functional but basic – a double bed, light, power point, blanket and the light cotton sleeping bag provided are all you need for a night in a concrete tube. The toilet and showers are a couple of minutes' walk away, details on booking.

To do

Visitors vary, from young backpackers and travellers looking for cheap accommodation to Dutch senior-citizen cyclists who know a bargain when they see one. Ottensheim has a beautiful location by the Danube and a castle. Details of places for breakfast, drinks and bathroom facilities are provided in the joining instructions.

Das Park Hotel
Ottensheim
Near Linz
Austria
online information only
www.dasparkhotel.net
Three double-room pipes

Rates and location There are currently three tubes, with an honesty box for contributions towards the upkeep. €20 would be an acceptable minimum for a night, but leaving €40 ensures that this art project can benefit the community and be developed at other locations. Ottensheim is a short taxi ride from nearby Linz, and the tubes are located in the Donauradweg park, next to the Danube.

Whitepod

Hi-tech igloos in Swiss eco resort

Whitepod is the creation of Swiss-born Sofia de Meyer, who wanted a high-tech solution to the challenge of creating a different, eco-friendly way of catching up with yourself in the natural beauty of the Swiss Alps.

Now in its third year, the resort has left little mark on the environment, but made a great mark in ecotourism – winning the Responsible Tourism Award for Innovation.

The twelve geodesic dome pods that make up Whitepod have been equipped with traditional furnishings and a simple wood-burning stove that keeps you comfortably warm. The pods are lit by lanterns and the only electricity is in the main chalet 3 or 4 minutes' walk away. Covered with white canvas in the winter and green in the summer, they blend perfectly into the surrounding landscape. The pods themselves are built on wooden platforms, so they can be moved easily. The main chalet houses the dining and spa facilities as well as the bathrooms, although the larger pavilion pods have en suite facilities.

The view of the mountains opposite, from the large bedroom window of the pod, is stunning, even more so when the sunlight reflects off the snow to wake you up in the morning. No need for an alarm clock here. After time on the private ski run with three lifts and 7 km (4 miles) of piste, or a traditional snow-shoe randonnée (ramble) in the nearby forests, you sleep soundly and wake early – but refreshed. Perhaps it is the clear mountain air or the fondue of the previous night, but you seem to have energy that was lacking when you arrived. This outdoor effort also builds up an appetite and the resident chef provides two nightly menus, one with traditionally hearty Swiss mountain food such as raclette and fondue, the other with lighter dishes using locally sourced ingredients. Such is the integration with the community, that Whitepod even runs a small grocery store for villagers.

WHITEPOD
Les Cerniers
Batt. Postale 681
1871 Les Giettes - Switzerland
+41 24 471 38 38
reservations@whitepod.com
www.whitepod.com
Twelve pods available

Rates
From 325 Swiss francs (200 €) to Christmas /
New Year pricing of Fr465 (280 €) for the "Expedition"
pod per night, based on single or double occupancy
and subject to a two-night minimum stay. The larger
Pavilion pods are from Fr585 (350 €) to Fr835
(500 €) at Christmas / New Year plus tax.

The main chalet provides an upstairs spa, offering massages and therapies. The Whitepod team also offer a number of non-ski outdoor activities including sledging – with the night sledge-run lit by torches particularly recommended. Equipment can be hired on site although guests should bring outdoor boots to walk on the snow and winter sports clothing. As with all winter resorts, you should bring high-factor sunscreen and sunglasses. Bring a swimsuit for the sauna too.

Location
The resort is above "Les Cerniers", a small village at the foot of the Dents du Midi. The nearest town is Aigle, where you should aim if you're travelling by train from Geneva, or if arriving by TGV.

Hôtel Palafitte

Hotel on stilts, in the heart of Switzerland

Although the Swiss are known worldwide for their fine chocolate and engineering excellence, unusual hotels do not immediately spring to mind. Hôtel Palafitte connects the quality tastes of the discerning Swiss, with something a little bit different – rooms built directly over Neuchâtel Lake, with private terraces and ladders dipping into the water for guests.

All the lakeside apartments are staggered so that they have an unobstructed view of the lake – from just about everywhere in the room – even the bath! Your privacy is assured as none of the rooms have direct views of the other rooms. The rooms themselves are impressively furnished with the latest gadgets, hi-tech TV, computer and sound systems. Don't forget to ask how everything works when you're shown your room otherwise you'll spend your evening reading manuals or calling reception for instructions.

The night view of the moon shimmering on the lake with the Alps in the distance is very impressive and the morning sunrise is stunning. While the rooms on the shore are perfectly adequate, it's worth the additional cost of the lakeside room to enjoy the view and private terrace.

Hôtel Palafitte
Route des Gouttes d'Or 2
Neuchâtel
CH-2000
Switzerland
+41 32 723 02 02
reservation@palafitte.ch · www.palafitte.ch
Twenty-four suites built directly over the lake

Rates and location Lakeside pavilions from 505 Swiss francs (US$415 / €300) to Fr680 (US$560 / €410). The shore-based pavilions are cheaper at Fr385–490 (US$320–410 / €235–300) but don't share the lake access from the terrace. The hotel is on the outskirts of the town, about 10 minutes to the main shopping area by public bus. The hotel provides a free shuttle bus for guests to and from the railway station.

To do

Neuchâtel, although a pretty town, is
better known as the heartland of the
Swiss watchmaking industry than as
a tourist destination. It is also famous
for the tasty fondue Neuchâteloise,
made from a mixture of Gruyère and
Emmental cheeses. While there are
several museums of history locally, we
recommend you check out the Wine
and Grape Museum housed in the
Château de Boudry, which gives the
story of the evolution of vine-growing
through the ages (+41 (0)32 842 1098).
Outside Neuchâtel in the surrounding
Jura mountains, there are plenty of pretty
alpine villages and the opportunity
to take boat and sailing trips on Lake
Neuchâtel itself. The hotel can make
suggestions and book activities for guests.

Iglu-Dorf

Sleep in an artist igloo or build your own!

Adrian Günter built his first igloo in 1996, to better enjoy the mountain and first powder snow of the day. Following an avalanche of interest from friends wanting to sample an igloo night, he increased the number of igloos and opened the "small world in white" in 2004, with five villages across Switzerland and Germany now accepting guests.

Moving 3,000 tons of snow every December to build each village, Adrian invites Inuit artists from Canada to craft sculptures inside each village. With only an ice pick, motor saw and shovel, artists produce seals, arctic wolves, polar bears and whales as well as swirling designs and patterns illuminated by candlelight to overlook the guests from the walls.

The villages are open from Christmas Day to the beginning of April each year, snow conditions permitting. With 5,600 visitors in 2006, all ages have enjoyed the cosy hospitality of an expedition sleeping bag and sheepskin rug, from the youngest 19-month-old baby to an 83-year-old lady guest.

A variety of igloo options are available in the different villages, from standard and group igloos to "Romantic" suites with private whirlpool or sauna. The team have even built a church, including an altar and baptismal font for a wedding party. Every village is equipped with a large igloo hotel lobby and bar where the evening meal of Gruyère fondue and mulled wine is served. The top-range "Romantic-plus" igloos include their own toilet, although you'll not want to spend too long sitting on the seat!

IGLU-DORF GmbH
Rotzbergstrasse 15
6362 Stansstad - Switzerland
+41 (0)41 612 27 28
info@iglu-dorf.com
www.iglu-dorf.com
Forty-two to sixty-two rooms,
 depending on the village

Rates Available in locations in the Swiss Alps and in Zugspitze, villages accommodate up to thirty-eight guests in different igloo options from standard and "Romantic" igloos for two, to larger family and group igloos. Prices are lowest midweek, rising at weekends and during the New Year. They include food, non-alcoholic beverages and the use of sauna or whirlpool facilities.

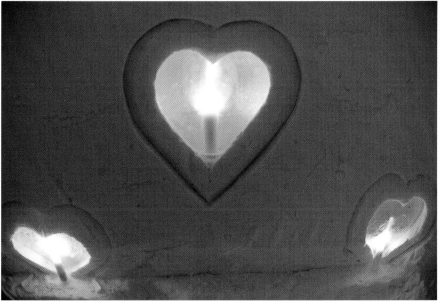

One night in the standard igloo is from
149 Swiss francs (€99) per person. The most
inexpensive romantic igloo can be booked for
Fr239 (€159) per person, while weekend nights
in the top-range "Romantic plus" suites cost
around Fr510 (€339) per person, per night.

Location
There are five IGLU-DORF locations, Davos – Klosters,
Engelberg, Gstaad and Zermatt in Switzerland, plus
Zugspitze in Germany. The largest in Zugspitze can
accommodate up to sixty-two guests.

To do

While the snowboarding and snowshoeing activities available at all the villages are to be expected, your overnight package includes the use of a communal sauna or whirlpool. After spending the day on the piste in the fresh mountain air, there are few things more relaxing than sitting in a whirlpool watching the sun set over the mountains.

For an additional fee, your mountain guide hosts also offer the chance to experience airboarding – an ultimate downhill ride on a hi-tech sledge, head first and inches off the snow. Those less inclined to high-adrenaline activity may instead want to learn how to build their own igloo block for block and experience the highlight of putting the last brick into your own snow house!

BelRepayre

American Airstream caravan retro chic in France

Perry and Coline, charming owners of the BelRepayre farmhouse, have created a hillside campsite that has become a mecca for Airstream owners in Europe. These polished aluminium caravans were the most stylish way to travel in 50s and 70s America and are overdue a revival if Perry has anything to do with it. The Airstreams are kept in good condition and they are much in demand, from visitors keen to sample this definition of retro chic as well as from film crews keen to provide on-location glamour and on-set period decor. Perry is an expert on restoration and the Airstreams have not only been lovingly restored, but they are furnished with period furniture, TV, cutlery and crockery. Melamine plates and salad servers anyone? You'll find them here, as well as some superb retro print fabrics that require sunglasses to tone down the lurid orange and brown stripes of the loungers, pink mock fur and shiny silver glitter-balls. If disco is your thing check out the Apollo Lounge, the bar / diner in a restored Airstream that becomes the focal point for summer evenings after the barbeques have died down. If you're lucky Perry will put on his clown costume and host a show in this most offbeat and groovy outdoor destination.

The Airstream caravans are entirely equipped for self-catering. Each caravan has its own awning or parasol, BBQ, outside tables, chairs and sunbeds. On the campsite you'll find a welcome desk with a little shop for basics including fresh bread, croissants and organic products from local farmers. The team also host a number of vintage rallies offering large flat pitches with water taps and electricity outlets.

BelRepayre
Ariège
Midi-Pyrenees
France
+33 (0)561 68 11 99
info@airstreameurope.com
www.airstreameurope.com
Seven caravans available for rent

Rates
Seven caravans are currently available for rental.
A single night in an Airstream for two is from €60
in low season to €100 for the larger four-berth
"Overlander" in high season. Discounts are available
for longer stays and for owners arriving in vintage
cars and towing vintage caravans.

To do

The campsite has ping-pong, table football and plenty of sports equipment to use in the fields adjoining the site. Perry also hosts outdoor movie nights, entertainment and shows from the Apollo bar. With a fantastic view of the Pyrenees mountains, there are several easy walks into the nearby Bélène forest. BelRepayre is in the heart of the Cathar region with its ninth-

to twelfth-century castles. The campsite is near a bison farm and the medieval town of Mirepoix, where you will find shops, banks, post office, supermarket, etc., plus fairs and festivals throughout the summer, is only 15 minutes' drive. The area is well served for outdoor activities including horseriding, bike hire, swimming and canoeing.

Location
BelRepayre is off autoroute A61 (exit 22 – Bram) or
A66 (exit Pamiers), in the foothills of the Pyrenees.
It's 90 km (55 miles) south of Toulouse, between
Carcassonne and Foix.

Les Hautes Roches

Sleep in caves with a gourmet restaurant

With twelve rooms carved out of the limestone rockface and a gourmet restaurant, Domaine des Hautes Roches opened its doors to guests in 1989. Formerly inhabited by the monks of the nearby Abbey of Marmoutier, they were renovated over the course of eighteen months by owner Philippe Mollard to become the first troglodyte hotel in France. These once-abandoned caves and adjoining seventeenth-century pavilion had lain dormant for nearly fifteen years. Now Les Hautes Roches represents a historic and sensible base from which to visit the most famous chateaux of the Loire Valley.

The caves themselves were dug out to quarry the light-coloured stone used to build some of the most famous chateaux of the surrounding area and became monk refuges during the wars of religion. Used on occasion for growing mushrooms as well as for ageing wine, from 1855 to 1975, the Domaine des Pentes was among the finest wine-producing properties of the Vouvray region, before serving as a storage area for a company dealing in spirits.

The hotel has twelve rooms in caves, plus three rooms in the pavilion building. The cave rooms themselves are not cut so deeply into the cliff face to be claustrophobic and benefit from large windows that bring light and an unobstructed view of the Loire opposite. While the cave rooms lack air-conditioning, during the summer months, they remain fairly cool, especially if curtains are drawn during the hottest part of the day. As the hotel faces the RN152, those expecting to open the windows for ventilation may be disappointed if they also wish for absolute peace and quiet, as the road can be busy.

Outside there are a number of grassed terraces and an open-air pool available for guest use in the high-season months.

The restaurant has received many excellent reviews and is situated in the small manor house, with large windows opening onto the river. Chef Didier Edon has been with the hotel for over ten years and offers high-quality gourmet cooking, specializing in seafood. Closed Mondays.

Les Hautes Roches
86 Quai de la Loire
Rochecorbon, 37210
France
+33 (0)2 47 52 88 88
hautesroches@relaischateaux.com
http://www.leshautesroches.com
Twelve cave rooms

Rates
Cave rooms on a double occupancy basis per night range from €160 for a small double to €270 for a larger deluxe room. The rate for continental breakfast is €19 per person.

Location
The hotel is on the outskirts of Rochecarbon which falls into the "appellation contrôlée" of the great wines of Vouvray. The historic city of Tours is only 8 km (5 miles) to the west.

To do

The Loire Valley is famous for castles and wine and both are within easy reach of the hotel. The great chateaux at Chenonceau, Blois, Cheverny, Azay-le-Rideau, Chambord, Chaumont and Amboise are all within a radius of 60 km (40 miles). We especially recommend the chateau of Villandry, 35 minutes away by car, for its world-renowned formal gardens. Guests might also be interested to join a Loire boat excursion that can be booked by the hotel, lasting around 45 minutes with commentary.

Le Carré Rouge

Sleep in a red cube with no running water or electricity

The Carré Rouge, a modern artwork by Gloria Friedmann, is a cube built with a red face to the south and a glazed face to the north. Lost in the middle of the French countryside, on the Langres plain, it's a superb site for an unusual romantic retreat, or for a family getaway.

The cube is organized on two levels: below you can cook and eat, and upstairs are three double beds.

As there's no running water or electricity, your stay there is a kind of return to nature that children will revel in: rainwater is recuperated via a water pump and drinking water comes from the village fountain, a few minutes' walk away (700 m)... As for lighting, oil lamps and candles are available while the wood-burning stove (no need to chop the wood yourself, it's kindly supplied) also heats the whole space via a central chimney.

Route de Santenoge 52160
Villars-Santenoge – Haute-Marne,
south of Plateau de Langres
Tel.: +33 (0)6 62 03 98 38
Fax: Solange Guenin at +33 (0)325 842 210
E-mail: jf.guenin@free.fr
www.leconsortium.com/carrerg

Rates and location €130 per weekend + €30 supplement per day (e.g. €190 four days), sleeps one to six people (max.). Sheets, quilts, covers, pillows, towels, dishes, wood for cooking and heating, and gas lamps are all supplied. By car from Paris, take the A5 exit Langres-sud and A6 exit Auxerre-sud. At Villars-Santenoge, follow signs to Chaugey. At the laundry, turn right on the track to Chalmandrier farm.

La Cabane Perchée

Treehouse in French château estate

Nestling 6 m up in the branches of an immense 100-year-old oak in the grounds of Château Valmer estate sits "La Cabane Perchée" treehouse. The nineteenth-century estate is mainly laid to vines, with a forest of trees bordering the 200 m of private beach for guests. Surrounding the chateau itself are more formal gardens with swimming pool and patio area. Purchased in 1949 by the parents of the current proprietors, the chateau has been continually upgraded from an out-of-town family residence to the four-star hotel that welcomes guests today. With forty-two rooms, restaurant, spa, sauna and hammam, the hotel is part of a portfolio of hotel properties overseen by the celebrated French chef Alain Ducasse, so you can be sure that the food won't disappoint. Ingredients include locally sourced fish as well as vegetables from the kitchen garden of the chateau.

The treehouse itself is reached by a small wooden staircase leading up to a comfortably sized balcony with space enough for two deckchairs, a couple of director chairs and a small table. It provides a good view of the chateau on one side and the sea on the other. Inside, the bedroom is simply furnished with a mosquito net covering the double bed. There's a small shower room and toilet alongside the bedroom. Food is taken in the chateau or in the beach bar.

Although the tree provides shade, the room can get hot during high summer days, although most guests will already be enjoying the facilities of the beach. The evening heat is much more relaxing and guests are sure to enjoy a glass of local rosé on the balcony as the sun goes down before dinner.

Hôtel Château Valmer
Route de Gigaro
83420 La Croix-Valmer
France
+33 (0)4 94 55 15 15
info@chateauvalmer.com
www.chateauvalmer.com
One double bedroom

Rates and location From €370 to €460. The spa facilities of the main hotel are available to treehouse guests with an additional charge for treatments. The chateau is 10 km from the resort of Saint-Tropez and 100 km from the international airport at Nice off the fast E80 / A8 autoroute. From Nice, take the sortie Saint-Tropez/Le Muy and then follow the RN98 and RD559 to La Croix-Valmer.

To do

La Croix-Valmer sits at the southern end of the Saint-Tropez peninsula, surrounded by vineyards with several really beautiful sandy beaches – plus the Domaine du Cap Lardier nature reserve which is perfect for hiking and bike rides. If Saint-Tropez is the place to see and be seen, then Croix-Valmer represents the low-key alternative for those who want to get away from the crowds. During the summer months, guests have access to the private beach of the hotel a few metres from the treehouse. The beach facilities include a tennis court, swimming pool and jacuzzi as well as sun loungers, deckchairs and parasols. In addition, the beach team can provide guests with pedalos, windsurfers and canoes. Book ahead to arrange jetskis and water skiing. The beach also has a small bar where you can order lunch and dinner from the main hotel restaurant. Outside the beach season, consider renting a mountain bike for trips along the coastline or to the nature reserve, or visit the centre of the perfume industry at Grasse, 85 km away.

Atelier sul Mare

Hotel-museum of modern art

The creation of Antonio Presti, who is quite a character, Atelier sul Mare is more than a hotel. Located halfway between Palermo and Messina, it's well worth a trip even if it's not the height of luxury.

When planning your trip, don't rely on the hotel website, which doesn't do justice to the place. Although the road you can see between the hotel and the beach does exist, it turns into a cul-de-sac after a short distance and is little used. On the other hand, the view is sublime: the water comes almost up to the windows and the Aeolian Islands form a magnificent and mysterious background.

The tone of the hotel is set at the entrance: Atelier sul Mare is totally given over to modern art. In contrast to many establishments calling themselves art hotels, here the word "art" is not taken in vain: each room has actually been designed by a different artist.

Of the forty rooms in the hotel, thirteen have been designed by modern artists. We particularly recommend the "Prophet's Room", in homage to Pier Paolo Pasolini (by Dario Bellezza, Adele Cambria, Antonio Presti), "Trinacria" (by Maurizio Staccioli) with its immense triangular bed, and

Atelier sul Mare
Via Cesare Battisti, 4
Castel di Tusa (Me) -Sicily - Italy
Tel.: +39 (0)921 334 295 - +39 (0)921 334 283
E-mail: ateliersulmare@interfree.it
www.ateliersulmare.it
Forty rooms - Thirteen art rooms

Rates and location
Located halfway between Palermo and Messina
Thirteen art rooms from €70 to €145 per person.

153

"Sigismond's Tower" (by Raoul Ruiz), in which the roof can be opened manually to let you sleep under the stars, spread-eagled on a vast round bed installed in the depths of a cylinder.

It should also be noted that Antonio Presti, in accordance with his social conscience, wanted to give the place a democratic character and make it accessible to the less well-off. So he has deliberately kept prices low (from €70 per person per night) and it's not unknown for him to offer one or two nights' hospitality to passing artists.

Antonio Presti

The son of a wealthy Sicilian cement manufacturer, Antonio Presti soon took a different direction and found his niche as troublemaker of the Sicilian art scene. Although threatened several times by the Mafia, Antonio has always held his own, claiming to want to "terrorize the terrorists". Today, thanks to his success and subsequent publicity, he's left alone and can concentrate on his main goal: the democratization of art. His first major project was at Catania in eastern Sicily: to help the residents of the dreary suburbs of the town see the relevance of art to their own lives, he had the bright idea of having giant portraits made of local residents by world-famous photographers.

These images were later hung directly on the façades of Catania social housing blocks and let residents gradually discover a certain sense of self-pride. In contrast to many projects of this nature, Antonio wanted at all costs to avoid the typical syndrome of modern art being brought to working-class suburbs and then, misunderstood by most people as something far removed from their own experience, taken away again, leaving behind little trace of its passage. Here, the residents truly feel at home with their art all around them.

After Atelier sul Mare, Antonio is now working on a new iconoclastic project: in a bid to draw attention to the impending ecological crisis in the river near Palermo station, with support in the media from Danielle Mitterrand, wife of the former French president, he brought along hundreds of children who symbolically poured into the river fresh water taken from the source upstream... Antonio now plans to install sculptures on the site, and as he says, these may be the first modern artworks ever to be displayed in an open sewer.

Things to do

If you're not troubled by vertiginous mountain roads, a walk around the Fiumara d'Arte sculpture park is highly recommended. Also created by Antonio Presti, it consists of a dozen or so artworks exhibited in the open air along a (long) mountain track. Allow a whole day for the trip. A map is available at hotel reception. If you're looking for something quieter, the celebrated and magnificent cathedral in the nearby town of Cefalù should be seen. The square in front of the cathedral is ideal for a snack or drink.

Marqués de Riscal

A stunning Gehry-designed hotel

A roofline of shimmering ribbons of pink, gold and silver titanium, the hotel Marqués de Riscal in the northern Spanish town of Elciego echoes the Gehry Associates trademark architecture found in the Guggenheim Bilbao and Bridge of Life building in Panama. The hotel was originally conceived as a twenty-first-century wine chateau in the Rioja Alavesa grape-growing region. It has been transformed into Frank O. Gehry's only hotel project to date.

Vinos de los Herederos de Marqués de Riscal is recognized as a pioneer in winemaking and the hotel is a futuristic beacon rising above the classical stone architecture of the town and the surrounding vineyards to highlight the growth in fortunes of the Rioja wine region as a whole.

The main Gehry-designed hotel has forty-three rooms and is stunning in every respect, both externally and internally, with designer furniture and hi-tech gadgets. There are also a number of more traditional, utilitarian rooms in an annex, connected to Hotel Marqués de Riscal by a bridge, where the spa and pool are located. Although the annex rooms have views of the vineyard and artistic furnishings, they lack the outrageous charm of the main building.

There are two restaurants in the hotel; "1860" and the more formal Marqués de Riscal restaurant which is closed on Mondays. While there have been mixed reviews for the more formal restaurant, the executive chef is the Michelin-starred Francis Paniego, so an average meal is unlikely and the wines will most certainly be exceptional.

The spa itself is worthy of mention for it provides wine therapy treatments using products made from grape extracts, created exclusively by Caudalíe Vinothérapie. It has received many awards for the treatments and venue. Now you can see, drink and be beautified with Rioja grapes.

Managed by Starwood Hotels and Resorts brand, "The Luxury Collection" Hotel Marqués de Riscal may appear a little out of the way, but is well worth the detour to take in the stunning design and wine-themed spa.

Hotel Marqués de Riscal
Calle Torrea, 1
Elciego 01340
Spain
+34 (0)945 180880
reservations.marquesderiscal@luxurycollection.com
www.luxurycollection.com
Forty-three rooms and suites

Rates From €300 for a grand deluxe room in low season to €850 in high season, exclusive of VAT but including breakfast. Suites are from €350 to €1,095 with the luxurious Gehry suite in addition.

Location Elciego is about 112 km (70 miles) south of the city of Bilbao.

To do

Elciego is near a number of medieval towns, where the traditions of hearty food and hospitality have never been lost. Take the "Ruta del Vino" tour by car to get a flavour of the region with regular tasting spots at smaller Rioja producers along the way. Many visitors will have arrived via Bilbao (112 km / 70 miles), visiting this rejuvenated Basque city and home to the famous Guggenheim Museum. Early July sees the famous bull-running in Pamplona (120 km / 75 miles) which although latterly a tourist haven is worth the spectacle.

Hotel Puerta América

Every floor a different design adventure

With twelve floors and communal spaces providing a unique style designed by nineteen design agencies, your choice of room is critical at Hotel Puerta América. Thankfully the front-desk staff anticipate guests changing rooms. A menu of design choices for the different floors is provided at check-in and you are recommended to study closely, or to review the website in advance. Some floors are a triumph of style over substance and there are stories of guests whose frustration in trying to dim the walls or use hi-tech appliances forced them to change rooms. Although floors have a similar layout, when you leave the elevator on each floor you feel in altogether different worlds – from futuristic red plastic to black marble through to traditional leather and wood.

Examples include the first floor by Zaha Hadid, where everything seems to come out from the wall. The bathroom is a single structure from floor to ceiling, which changes colour according to the room. Most frustratingly, the waste basket is a challenge for guests because it's not so easy to find. Or you can just drop your rubbish on the floor ...

The eighth floor by Kathryn Findlay, "Light in Motion", intends to suggest a feminine touch. Refusing to consider walls or doors, Findlay provided for sweeping white curtains that separate the bathroom from the room. The entire room is white and forms a single space.

Patience is required on the ninth floor with Richard Gluckman's "Boxes of Colours" concept as you need to look for everything, all hidden in boxes. The biggest box, in the middle of the room, houses the TV. In the bathroom, the first thing you see when you enter is a large glass box containing the shower, with a sliding door separating it from the bedroom and a white metal curtain. A raw industrial look contrasts with back-lit illumination, so don't forget to ask how to turn off the lights otherwise you'll struggle to get to sleep.

With every floor a different artistic design, this hotel challenges the senses in an architectural assault course of design.

Hotel Puerta América
Avenida de América, 41
28002 Madrid ·
Spain
+34 (0)917 445 400
hotel.puertamerica@hoteles-silken.com
www.hotelpuertamerica.com
342 bedrooms

Rates
The Hotel Puerta América has 342 bedrooms including a number of suites on the twelfth floor. You should expect to pay around €360 for a double room plus 7% tax excluding breakfast.

To do

While there is a pool and spa treatment room advertized at Puerta América, these are not major features of the hotel. There isn't much to visit locally, so you need to be prepared to take a taxi into town for restaurants and entertainment. Madrid has many world-class art galleries from traditional to modern. The Prado museum is a popular choice, and we recommend you consider hiring one of their professional guides (about €40) for the added interest of learning the background to the paintings.

Location
The hotel is midway between the airport and the city centre and is not in the centre of town. A taxi from the airport should cost around €15, and around €10 into town. Alternatively consider the metro stop next to the hotel, but be prepared to change a couple of times to get into the centre.

Hostel Celica

Former prison transformed into funky art house hostel

Following the departure of the Yugoslav army in 1991, it took until July 2003 for this former prison to be turned into the hostel and art centre complex that greets visitors today. Due to the slow bureaucracy of the former Yugoslavia, transferring ownership of these former army barracks from government ministries to the peoples' collective set up to run the hostel by the city of Ljubljana was a surprisingly lengthy undertaking. However, the patience and tenacity of the artists who have supported this project has finally been repaid with a well-admired conversion to a 'funky, hip' hostel that is the recipient of many accolades for the cell rooms and overall hospitality.

There are twenty cell rooms on the first floor, each decorated by a different artist. Some have added mezzanine bunk beds to use the small room space efficiently and most have retained the prison window bars for an authentic confinement feel. None of the cells are en suite, however the toilets upstairs are clean and functional, if not a little busy in the mornings.

The attic space has apartments with en suite facilities, but they aren't in the cell style and may get noisy if there's a band playing in the café. Live music is usually on Tuesdays, and the hostel bar serves keenly priced beer that helps to attract a friendly artist and commune subculture which is lively until late at night – or early in the morning at weekends. Pack earplugs if you're a light sleeper, or if your room is near the café.

Breakfast is provided in a glass-covered terrace, as is a much in-demand internet link that can be provided in cells for an additional charge. The restaurant is open for light snacks during the day, but with the centre of town only 10 minutes' walk away, most guests eat out at the many local cafés and restaurants at some time during their stay.

Hostel Celica
Metelkova 8
SI – 1000 Ljubljana
Slovenia
+ 386 (0)1 230 97 00
www.hostelcelica.com
Twenty cells plus dormitory, suites and disabled access room

Rates
There are a total of twenty-nine rooms, including suites and dormitories in the attic space and a room with disabled access on the ground floor. Some of the twenty cell rooms are for two occupants, and others have three beds. Prices for two-bed cells are from €23 in low season, and three-bed cells from €18, all per person per night. Guests

are additionally required to pay a nightly sales tax of €1.01 per person. There are minimum-stay requirements at peak periods and a single-occupancy supplement.

Location

Hostel Celica is in the heart of Ljubljana, just 300 m from the central rail and bus station and approximately 700 m from the city centre (Prešeren Square and old town). If you're arriving by air to Brnik Airport, there is a bus service to Ljubljana main bus station, around 5 minutes' walk from the hostel.

To do

Hostel Celica is situated in "Metelkova City", a new cultural area with galleries, artists' studios, library, cultural events and a vivid weekend party life. The hostel provides a free guided tour every day at 2 pm to showcase the cell rooms. If you've checked out their web tour and want to stay in a particular room, you shouldn't leave it to the guided tour to make your

choice known as the most popular cells are booked well in advance. The hostel also provides a booking service for adventure activities including white-water rafting on the Sava River – host to the world wild-water canoe and kayak championships. You can also try canyoning or, if getting wet isn't your thing, hire a bike to tour the local countryside.

Woodlyn Park

Sleep in a plane that fought in the Vietnam war

While many readers will have fallen asleep on a long flight, few can claim to have slept in a converted Bristol freighter plane. If two self-catering apartments in a 1950s plane weren't enough, Woodlyn Park also offers accommodation in a converted railway carriage and underground rooms carved into the hillside.

The plane was originally constructed in the UK and was one of the last Allied warplanes to see enemy action in Vietnam. Sustaining flak damage, it was eventually purchased by Woodlyn Park proprietor Billy Black, who with his customary enthusiasm set about its restoration. Now converted into two apartments, it offers vacation and overnight rental in a choice of tail or cockpit configurations.

Likewise, the Waitomo Express, a converted 1950s railcar, offers self-contained accommodation for groups of up to six in three separate rooms.

The latest addition, while promoted as Hobbit lodging, is more in keeping with two normally furnished apartments built into a hillside, with the addition of a turf roof. Perhaps, like the train and plane, these apartments will soon gain a more complete character and provide Hobbit features inside too …

Woodlyn Park is currently adding a boat, The Motunui, as a future accommodation attraction, with a dry dock being built on its own private island.

To do

Billy Black works hard to keep visitors amused here. Providing a sometimes hilarious Kiwi culture show as well as hire onsite of U-drive jet boats, Billy and his team provide a welcome injection of irreverent fun and showmanship to the otherwise relaxed pace of life in this area.

Woodlyn Park
1177 Waitomo Valley Road
RD7, Otorohanga
New Zealand
+64 (0)7878 6666
billy@woodlynpark.com.nz
www.woodlynpark.com.nz
Seven themed accommodation rentals

Rates With seven themed offerings available from NZ$115 (US$ 90) for couples sharing the train to NZ$145 (US$ 115) for accommodation in either Hobbit lodging or plane cockpit.

Location Woodlyn Park is between Auckland and Te Kuiti off the SH3. The park is about 5 minutes from the Waitomo Caves village tourist location.

The Boot Bed'n'Breakfast

Sleep in a boot

Creating a giant boot guesthouse on a 2.5 hectare property is perhaps the genius of an eccentric, and rather than convert an existing building, Steve Richards designed The Boot from scratch. With curved walls and ceilings, everything had to be custom fitted into carefully planned spaces. The result is an unusual, romantic hideaway – in the shape of a giant boot!

Provided are a queen-size double bed, facilities for hot drinks, a mini bar and bathroom with shower – building regulations require that there cannot be a kitchen. A continental or cooked breakfast is delivered from the nearby Jester House café to be enjoyed in the cosy bedroom, outside terrace or downstairs lounge. A supper platter can also be ordered for couples who relish the privacy, as many find when they arrive that they really don't want to go out. With a fireplace and underfloor heating, The Boot is open year round, mainly to tourists in the summer months, but with steady bookings from knowledgeable locals keen for a relaxing break during the rest of the year.

When Steve and partner Judy first created The Boot in 2001 they were considered slightly mad, but after several years of happy visitors they are rightly taking their place as local celebrities and contributing to the tapestry of attractions and folklore of this inspiring region.

Judy and Steve Richards
Jester House Estate
Coastal Highway, Tasman
Nelson, New Zealand
+64 (0)3 526 6742
jesters@ts.co.nz
www.theboot.co.nz
One double room

Rates
The double bedroom can be booked for NZ$ 250.00 (US$ 200), per couple per night, including breakfast and tax. Discounts for multiple nights are available, including weekends.

To do

Visitors are generally drawn to this region
by the Abel Tasman and Kahurangi
National Parks that have been given
World Heritage site status. The beaches
of Kina and Ruby Bay offer beautiful,
long and relaxing walks, swimming or
just lazing in the sun. Equally popular is
the seaside village of Mapua, a favourite
dinner destination. Mapua wharf has
three acclaimed restaurants, a gallery and
tours of the Waimea estuary by sea kayak
or jetboat. The Boot is also close to Nelson

home to the World of Wearable Art Gallery
and the next door Classic Car Gallery.
The stunning creations on display and
footage of their annual awards gives new
meaning to "dressing up" (www.wowcars.
co.nz). Next door to The Boot itself, the
Jester House café has become a much-
loved coffee stop serving breakfast, lunch
and snacks. The estate also has a garden,
children's maze and a tame eel attraction,
offering feeding during summer
months from September until May.

Location
Nearby Tasman is located between Nelson City
and the Abel Tasman and Kahurangi National Parks
at the top of the South Island of New Zealand.
It is around 35 minutes' drive from either Nelson
airport, or Nelson harbour for ferry connections
to North Island.

Wild Canopy Reserve

Treehouses and a Tree Suite to view the surrounding nature reserve

Originally an old rubber plantation, Wild Canopy Reserve (WCR) grew out of a wish to develop tourism in the Nilgiri area. For over forty years, the family team has converted the property into a fine wildlife reserve, now adding guest facilities and tree-house accommodation. The first treehouse was built in November 2004 and in 2006 a larger two-bedroom "Tree Suite" with bathrooms at different levels was added. The treehouse provides a view of the waterhole, lit by a remote-controlled light. The suite provides an impressive view of the surrounding thorny scrub jungle with a backdrop of the Nilgiri mountains. More tree suites are being added in 2007.

Wildlife is abundant and guests can see elephant, tiger, leopard, sloth bear, spotted and sambhar deer, wild boar as well as numerous birds according to your patience, season and luck!

The team encourages ecologically friendly and sustainable methods, including solar power, and is making efforts to reduce the need for modern transport. They are even considering how to bring back elephants for transport. The employment of staff from local indigenous communities is welcome too.

In the treehouses insect-proof nets are used on the beds and it is advisable to wear insect repellent suitable for the tropics. WCR is a dry region and they don't have leeches but they spray natural and indigenous repellents to keep snakes and other reptiles away. Under normal circumstances snakes are shy and don't cause trouble, so guests shouldn't be unduly alarmed. All guests are advised of basic precautions in the "RULES OF THE ROOST"

Wild Canopy Reserve
Bokkapuram
Masinagudi PO
Nilgiri Dist.
Tamil Nadu, India
+91 (0)423 2526034
bookings@wildcanopyreserve.com
www.wildcanopyreserve.com

Rates
The treehouse is from 5,000 rupees (US$ 125 / € 95) per couple per night in low season rising to 6,000 (US$ 150 / € 110) in high season. Buffet-style full board food and drink is an additional 1,000 rupees (US$ 25 / € 20) with taxes and tips in addition.

To do

To take best advantage of the trekking and wildlife-watching facilities, bring stout boots and pack pale and neutral shades of light cotton clothing. Weather is either wet / dry / mild, reaching a maximum of 25 °C in February and May, and dropping to 15 °C in December and January. A small torch is a good idea, as well as some light rain gear. Don't forget to bring binoculars!

Location

Wild Canopy Reserve is located on the edge of the Mudumalai National Park and Tiger Reserve in Tamil Nadu, at the intersection of the Karnataka and Kerala state borders. If a drive through countryside and forests isn't enough adventure for you, consider arriving at Coimbatore airport and taking the 3 hour train ride to Mettupalaiyam, then transferring to the rack and pinion Nilgiri mountain railway to travel to Ooty. The WCR team can then pick you up from Ooty, which is about an hour from the reserve. It doesn't take much more time than driving – but is more fun!

Hotel of Modern Art (HOMA)

Man-made sculpture amidst the natural wonders of Guilin region

You cannot fail to appreciate the outdoor sculptures surrounding the Hotel of Modern Art (HOMA) outside Guilin. The grounds of the hotel complex are home to the Yuzi Paradise sculpture park, housing a collection of modern art and sculpture built up since 1996. Over 200 sculptures are arranged in 530 hectares (1,300 acres) of parkland, against the stunning backdrop of the mountainous Guilin terrain.

HOMA has two hotel buildings, plus an art gallery and separate restaurant. One is a joint venture with the Relais and Chateaux and is much more art-oriented and inside the park itself. The other building (HOMA "Heart"), is a short walk away, near the entrance of Yuzi Paradise itself. The common areas of the buildings are spacious and the R+C property is decorated in a design-led style. The bedrooms however aren't particularly impressive, with small but functional bathrooms. It is externally where the resort scores highly. The Don Quixote building is the largest restaurant, although sometimes reserved for conference functions. The building is a quarter-sphere in shape and the curved exterior wall of glass provides a view of sunset in the evening. The reflecting pool outside the restaurant only serves to make the curves more impressive as the shadows lengthen. Equally impressive is the International Art Centre's triangular buildings and grass-topped roofs, intended to visually represent the Earth's continental shelves and intersecting plates. If only bedrooms had views of these beautiful buildings or more of a design theme themselves, their average facilities might be forgiven.

Hotel of Modern Art (HOMA)
Yuzi Paradise
Dabu Town, Yanshan District
Guilin 541006
People's Republic of China
yuzi@yuzile.com
www.yuzile.com
167 rooms in two buildings

Rates
There are 167 rooms in total across both hotel buildings, ranging from a standard room costing 1,080 yuan (US$ 150) to HOMA deluxe rooms at 2,880 yuan (US$ 300). There are an additional thirty-two suites and family rooms.

Location
Yuzi Paradise is halfway between Guilin and
Yangshuo (40 km / 25 miles) and around 45 minutes
by car from the airport at LiangJiang. While you can
arrange transportation yourself (there are buses
from Guilin and Yangshuo to Yuzi Paradise/Dabu
Town), we recommend arranging a transfer with
the hotel direct.

To do

The hotel and Yuzi Paradise grounds are recognized by the World Tourism Organization Forum as a specific "Scenic Spot". If your schedule allows, we suggest you ask for a picnic at reception and hire a bike to view the grounds of the sculpture park. Unlike most destinations in China where Western faces draw a crowd of interested onlookers, the park is a peaceful and welcome break from the tourist scene. There is also a recently opened spa, although most visitors are more likely to want to visit the Guilin area than stay on-site for too long. The picturesque town of Yangshuo is about 45 minutes' drive away for the popular boat trips on the Li River. Be prepared to be among the parade of tourists making this trip however. Although you're assured of at least one English speaker at the hotel to book trips, the prices reflect this and you might consider booking direct with one of the agencies in Yangshuo.

Benesse House

Like a science fiction film set…

Benesse House is an incredible place. In a setting that hovers between James Bond in Dr No and the TV series The Prisoner, your stay here is bound to be one of the best memories of your trip.

Built by the celebrated Japanese architect Tadao Ando, Benesse House opened in 1995 and has evolved constantly ever since.

In a building that serves as a museum for the modern art collection of Japanese multimillionaire Nobuko Fukutake, Tadao Ando has created a dozen or so rooms that form part of the museum itself. One great advantage is that, once the visitors have left for the day, the building is at your disposal and you can wander freely among the artworks. In fact, to reach the restaurant (featuring a painting by Basquiat) from your room, you have to pass through the museum…

Other than works worthy of any international museum (Giacometti, Jasper Johns, Sam Francis, Jackson Pollock, David Hockney…), some of the art is exhibited in the open air right down to the beach, where there is a jacuzzi… Useable at night, this faces an extraordinary desert-like volcanic island which adds to the mysterious and enigmatic nature of the place. Just so that you don't miss anything, when the tide is high swimming is a real delight.

From the different types of room on offer, the top choices are those in the "Oval". Access is by a little private monorail, like something out of a science fiction film, especially at night when the waning light of the carriage lamp illuminates the surroundings like the eye of a Cyclops. Once you're up there, the entrance to the famous Oval is spectacular: concealed inside the walls surrounding a small oval space, six doors lead to the bedrooms. Above, the enclosure is open to the sky, creating a real architectural work of art. From the rooms, the sea view is superb and the traditional hi-tech Japanese toilets will delight fans of technological gadgetry.

Gotanji, Naoshima-cho
Kagawa-gun, Kagawa
Japan 761-3110
Tel.:+81 87 892 2030
E-mail: naoshima@mail.benesse.co.jp
www.naoshima-is.co.jp/english/benessehouse/
guestroom/index.html

Six rooms in the "Oval": double room from 38,000 yen (€ 240) to 75,000 yen (€ 475)
Ten rooms in the Museum: double room from 34,650 yen (€ 220) to 75,000 yen (€ 475)
Seven other rooms in the "Park" and "Beach".
We recommend staying at least two nights.

Chichu: the most beautiful museum in the world?

In 2002, a few minutes' walk from Benesse House, Tadao Ando built a dream museum. An exceptional piece of architecture to house eight artworks, no more, no less: four sublime water-lily canvases by Monet, three works by James Turrell and an astonishing piece by Walter de Maria, Time/Timeless/No Time. The presentation of the Monet paintings is impressive, in a totally white room in which the floor is covered with thousands of mosaic fragments. We won't say any more about Turrell's exceptional Open Field so as not to spoil the surprise. Twice a week, on Friday and Saturday evenings, don't miss the Open Sky performance, one of the three other works by the American artist.

Things to do

The island of Naoshima, 5 minutes by car, is also a venue for experimental modern art that would be a pity to miss: a dozen works are scattered around the main village of the island. While you're there, don't miss the town of Kurashiki (about 40 minutes from the embarkation point for Naoshima), where we strongly recommend staying at the Ryokan Kurashiki. This is one of the most beautiful traditional hostels in Japan and a night spent there is a real traveller's experience in its own right.

From Europe to Naoshima without taking the plane

If you're coming from Europe and have some time to spare, an unforgettable means of getting to Naoshima Island is to take the Trans-Siberian Railroad from Moscow. Choose the more spectacular route through Mongolia and, once you've arrived in Beijing, have yourself a massage and spend the night in a good traditional hotel, such as the Red Capital Residence. The next day, take the night train to Shanghai, from where a boat leaves for Osaka, which is only 4 hours from Naoshima. Altogether you'll have travelled from Moscow to Naoshima without stepping on a plane, in less than a fortnight – and what a memorable experience

Capsule Hotels

Sleep in coffin-sized capsules

Capsule hotels, scattered around the larger towns in Japan, remain a major – and unusual – attraction for most foreign visitors. For the Japanese, on the other hand, their exotic appeal is less obvious: capsule hotels are mainly used by men (women are banned from most of them) after drinking too much on a night out, as happens regularly in Japan, even (especially) among work colleagues, and then missing the last train home to the suburbs. For foreigners, the capsules are an experience not to be missed…

Although the quality of the facilities can vary greatly (cleanliness, presence of a sauna, sometimes a luxurious spa, etc.) the basic elements are always the same: low prices (even if € 20–30 per night may seem relatively expensive for a coffin-sized compartment), a capsule whose dimensions are calculated to the nearest centimetre, metal lockers where you can leave your belongings overnight (it's clearly out of the question to take a suitcase into your capsule, unless you're reconciled to a sleepless night) – and that's all.

How you get inside the capsule may come as a surprise: for those not at ground level, you just climb up the ladder and slide (we use the term advisedly) inside. Amazingly, you're almost comfortable: you can turn around fairly easily (but avoid sudden movements…), even if you can't sit up. Inside are all the mod cons: television, a lamp with dimmer switch, a comfortable quilt, pillows, and of course a little curtain that should be drawn shut to isolate yourself from the outside world. Rest assured, this is Japan: although in theory anyone could open the capsule from the outside, cases of antisocial behaviour are extremely rare and you can count on spending the night undisturbed.

The one important item to remember is your earplugs. On the small TV screen inside the capsule, several porn channels are usually available. Many Japanese are rather keen on these, and your neighbour is only separated from you by a few centimetres of plastic…

Several addresses in most large Japanese towns
List available at: http://www.links.net/vita/trip/
japan/lodging/capsulehotel/
or http://gojapan.about.com/cs/accommodation/
a/tokyocapsule1.htm (supply the town name for
addresses outside Tokyo)

Rates
€ 20-30 per night

Niassam Hills Lodge

Rooms in a baobab tree

Niassam Hills Lodge is extraordinary, in the real sense of the word. In an isolated area of Senegal on the remarkable Siné Saloum delta, it is particularly well located facing a lagoon and an island covered in magnificent baobabs.

The site alone is worth a visit: although the official journey time from Dakar is 3½ hours, it frequently takes as long as 5 or 6 hours, depending on the state of your vehicle and the usually horrendous traffic out of Dakar, notably when nearing Rusfique, the nightmare of all Senegalese drivers. You may after all be pleased about your plane's arrival time (most European flights land in the middle of the night), as it means you'll miss all the traffic jams.

The yellow and black taxis that you'll find at the airport are sometimes in a dreadful state. Even though these shortcomings are offset by the legendary kindness (the justly famous teranga) of the Senegalese, we nevertheless advise you to arrange for a car to be sent from the lodge.

The hotel itself consists of thirteen rooms: four perched in the baobab trees and four on stilts, while the others are more classic and thus less interesting. The decor of the baobab and stilt rooms is a great success: wood, traditional furniture, mosquito net. The setting is enchanting: whether viewed from a hammock on one of the balconies outside a baobab room, or from an armchair on the little terrace of one of the rooms on stilts looking directly out over the water, the landscape is splendid and the atmosphere conducive to meditative daydreaming. If they're available, go for the two rooms on stilts located on the little private island, accessible by means of walkways across the water …

With plenty of bandes dessinées (comic strip albums) in the library, a swimming pool (not quite as satisfactory as the rest but especially suitable for children), very decent cuisine, and kayaks available, all in all you'll have a fantastic stay here.

Don't miss the excursions organized by the lodge, especially the full-day trip by pirogue in the Siné Saloum delta. The "aperitif" is unforgettable: all along the mangrove swamps, your guides collect oysters that cling naturally to the roots of the trees. Cooked on wood fires and accompanied by a squeeze of lemon and a glass of (good) Muscadet, even those who don't usually like raw oysters will find these divine.

Palmarin Ngallou, BP 08 JOAL
Senegal
Tel.: +221 (0)669 63 43
E-mail: niassam@hotmail.com
www.niassam.com

Rooms in baobab trees or on stilts: around € 85 per person, dinner and breakfast included.

To do

To round off your week in Senegal, avoid Saly with its tourist-packed reserves and instead visit the Tama Lodge at M'Bour beach, offering a beautiful African decor, a very pleasant restaurant and a clean beach, perfect for playing football with the Senegalese who flock here from 4 pm onwards, once the day begins to cool down.

Also avoid the Pierre de Lisse hotel-restaurant at Popenguin, which despite being recommended by all the tourist guides seemed very mediocre to us. On your way back to Dakar a detour via Gorée is indispensable: be sure to spend a night there to soak up the atmosphere of the island after the day-trippers have taken the boat back to Dakar around 5 pm. Stay at the charming Chevalier de Bouffiers hostelry, which also has the most pleasant restaurant on the island.

Hippo Point Wildlife Sanctuary Tower

Pagoda folly in the middle of a wildlife sanctuary

This delicate 40 m Kenyan cypress-clad pagoda stands 12 m wide at its base and offers four double rooms and a single inside the nine-storey construction. Nestling within the surrounding yellow acacia "fever" trees that surround much of Lake Naivasha, the design is completely accepted by wildlife, fooling short-sighted hippos to think that the tower is part and parcel of the landscape, a towering yellow acacia itself. It offers close-up views of monkeys, birds, giraffe, impala, zebra and of course the hippos that give the place its name. Completed in 1993, Dodo's tower is the eccentric folly of Dodo Cunningham-Reid, who wanted to build something special in Kenya.

Originally planned as a weekend escape for Dodo and husband Michael when visiting their 250 hectare Nderit estate, there is impressive attention to detail. The top of the tower provides a 360 degree observation lookout, while a floor below is a minaret-style meditation room, furnished with big cushions and a surround view. The middle tiers of the tower offer bedrooms with crisp Russian linens and covered verandas. Down spiral stairs you reach a mahogany-panelled lounge and drawing room, spectacularly original yet luxuriously functional.

Welcoming guests for an overnight stay or personalized rental, the tower and its staff cater for guests to enjoy their day at a leisurely pace. Perhaps breakfast on the veranda, hippo-watching while sipping English tea and freshly squeezed juices, or maybe a walk among the animals of the wildlife sanctuary itself. An afternoon might be spent on the lake in the beautiful teak Riva motorboat before a candle-lit gourmet dinner using foods from their on-site organic garden or fresh from the nearby farms. Such is the harmonious way that Hippo Point Tower integrates guest activities with the wildlife of the estate, you could perhaps forget that the 500 wallowing hippos peacefully waggling their ears in the lake are each two tons of wild animal. Given the protection that the estate affords the animals, they are very relaxed in human company and respectful of the guest presence, allowing a close-up experience of them in their natural habitat that is as unique as it is rewarding. A magical place.

Hippo Point Private Estate and Wildlife Sanctuary
PO Box 1852
Naivasha
Kenya
+ (254) 733333014
hippo-pt@africaonline.co.ke
www.hippo-pointkenya.com
Five luxuriously appointed rooms

Rates and location From US$ 550 (€ 400) per person per night, with trips tailored to individual requirements. As a luxurious alternative for a special occasion, this Garden of Eden retreat offers a magical beauty. 80 miles (150 km - 2 hours) from Nairobi on recently paved roads, or consider a private plane charter, taking only 25 minutes from Nairobi by light aircraft.

217

To do

Guests have unrestricted access to
the property and its surroundings.
Fishing, water sports and riding
can be arranged, as can game
drives at nearby private reserves.
The wildlife surrounding the
tower itself is worthy of mention,
with giraffes walking outside your
window and impala feeding on
the surrounding grasses. Both
leopard and the shy nocturnal
aardvark can often be spotted on
night game drives. The nearby
mock-Tudor Hippo Point house
has a fine 20 m swimming pool
and seven additional bedrooms for
larger groups. The pool is superbly
maintained and would not be out
of place in a luxury hotel or spa
much closer to civilization, but
echoes the style that personifies
the Cunningham-Reid approach of
doing things properly or not at all.

About the author

Setting up www.UnusualHotelsOfTheWorld.com with friend Simon Penn in 2004 to catalogue memorable properties to stay, Steve Dobson has built a team of fun loving travel contributors keen to share their notes of the most interesting and unusual places around the world.

Juggling the demands as a father to two small children, Steve travels to far-flung destinations whenever budget or childcare allow.

He is 40, loves to cook and has a hammock in the garden which he hopes to enjoy if the UK weather ever gets warm enough.

Acknowledgements

To Kirsty, Oliver and Arran for their patience and support. To Simon for the shared inspiration. For their perspiration and persistence - Sid, Vikram, Hemant and the gounusual.com development team. You are all welcome to share space on my hammock!

JONGLEZ PUBLISHING
TRAVEL OFF THE BEATEN TRACKS

In English

Secret bars & restaurants in Paris
Secret Brussels
Secret French Riviera
Secret Paris
Secret Provence
Secret Rome
Unusual hotels of the world
Unusual shopping in Paris

In French

Banlieue de Paris insolite et secrète
Boutiques insolites à Paris
Bruxelles insolite et secret
Côte d'Azur insolite et secrète
Hôtels insolites
Marseille insolite et secret
Rome insolite et secret
Paris bars & restos insolites
Paris méconnu
Provence insolite et secrète
Un soir insolite à Paris

In Italian

Alberghi insoliti nel mondo
Parigi insolita e segreta
Roma insolita e segreta